Bridal Shower Guidebook

How to Host a
Successful Bridal Shower

MYRA M. ISHEE

JM Publications
A Division Of
JM PRODUCTIONS
BRENTWOOD, TN 37027

ISBN: 0-939298-44-9

Printed in the United States of America

Acknowledgments

I was richly blessed during the writing of this book by having the gracious assistance and helpful editorial suggestions of my son, Mark, whose expert skills were invaluable at all stages of this project.

Also, I am deeply grateful to my husband, John, for his encouragement and support.

Lovingly dedicated to my parents,
Virginia and Norris Miles

Contents

Preface

Parties for the bride and her attendants have always been sparkling, sentimental occasions. The practical, popular custom of giving "showers" lingers, often in luncheons for the bride or joint showers for the bride and groom. The bridal shower, in addition to being a social event, is useful and fun even for the bride who seemingly has "everything."

No form of party is nicer or more enjoyable — for the hostess, for the guest of honor, or for the guests — than the shower. It is a party for close friends as well as an occasion in honor of someone you love, and provides an opportunity for intimacy, fun, and informality. No party is more fun to plan than a shower. Also, it is the easiest and most satisfying of all forms of entertaining if it is properly planned in advance. Additionally, it offers the hostess a chance to be creative and imaginative. The theme for a shower may be almost anything — a coffee, luncheon, or afternoon tea for "ladies only." It may also be a dinner or evening party where the bridegroom and his friends are included.

Although there are certain traditions and customs associated with bridal showers, there are no basic rules or procedures to be followed. The customs of one's own community should serve as the primary guide in planning any shower. This book will help you to create and to plan memorable showers, but it is not so much a "rulebook" as it is an "idea book." Adapt the suggestions within to meet your special needs and circumstances. *The Bridal Shower Guidebook* is designed to help the hostess who wants to honor a friend with a shower, and who seeks new and different shower ideas in addition to more common, conventional ones. By combining selected portions of the shower ideas presented within, any hostess can create an enjoyable and original shower.

I hope that the many suggestions presented in this book will be of help to anyone who plans to give or attend a shower, as well as to the engaged girl and her family during this happy period of her life.

Myra M. Ishee
June, 1985

Planning

A bridal shower should be planned well in advance, and down to the last detail. As in preparing for other memorable parties, showers are the result of creative ideas and planning as well as special attention given to the guests, the circumstances, and the time. There are formal and informal parties, indoor and outdoor ones, and parties that move freely from living room to lawn and back again. A shower may involve a full-scale meal, a morning coffee, an afternoon tea, a late evening supper, or just dessert and coffee. Often, the food is no more than light refreshments or an assortment of snacks with a beverage. Successful bridal showers depend less upon the money spent than upon the creativity and ingenuity with which the party is planned. If planning the shower is fun for the hostess, carrying out her plans will likewise be fun for the guests.

Although their looks and manners tend to change with the years, the whole round of pre-wedding parties varies depending on the type of wedding, the local customs, and the tastes and circumstances of the bride and groom. The number of showers given should be limited, in order to spare the bride's time and her friends' budgets. Although not as common as the bridal shower, there is no reason why the ushers or a close friend cannot give a shower for the groom. The theme of such a shower would of course be masculine — perhaps a workshop shower or a sports shower.

The best time to hold any shower is a month or more before the wedding day. A lasting benefit of such pre-wedding events is that both sides of the family and their friends become acquainted, possibly for the first time. By the time the wedding day arrives, everyone feels more relaxed and can therefore be more congenial and friendly at the wedding.

Traditionally, bridal showers are friendly gatherings of intimate friends, held to honor the bride and "shower her with gifts." A recent custom which has become widespread of giving enormous parties — sometimes including every guest on the wedding list, and often including mere acquaintances — is in very poor taste and is contrary to the spirit of the traditional bridal shower. Such affairs are an obvious bid for gifts, and totally ignore the intimacy and friendship which are the charm of a true shower.

Who Hosts Showers?

The hostess is usually a close friend of the bride-to-be, and will give one of the bride's most essential showers. Or she may wish to entertain the prospective bride, but must do so after a number of showers have already been given, in which case the hostess will be as concerned with originality as with practicality. There will also be times when it is desirable to entertain both bride and groom.

It is often a good idea for two or three people to jointly host a shower rather than have too many showers, which can become a financial inconvenience for guests who are invited to several parties for the same person. When several friends of the bride host the shower together, the responsibility and expense of invitations, decorations, hostess gift, and refreshments are shared. One or two showers is a sensible limit, and each can be planned for a different group. *The Bridal Shower Guidebook* provides numerous suggestions for all these occasions.

Members of the immediate family, including mother, sister, or grandmother of either the bride or groom should not act as hostess, although they may share the facilities of their home, or provide monetary assistance. Exceptional circumstances may alter this; for example, if the bride is from a foreign country, and knows no one but the groom and his family, they may properly plan a shower for her.

Theme: What Kind of Shower Will It Be?

A specific theme simplifies planning, providing a focal point for all the party elements. Special days (Christmas, Valentine's Day, Easter, Fourth of July) have simple, colorful built-in themes. Endless opportunities exist for festive affairs. Themes for these varied occasions may be keyed to the seasons or to the purpose of the gathering, or even to a favorite hobby or avocation of the person for whom the celebration is being given.

The hostess and the bride select a mutually convenient date, and then decide what kind of shower is most appropriate — kitchen, linen, etc. The hostess may want to notify the guests on the invitations about the couple's choice of decor and color preferences to aid them in their selection of gifts.

Guests: Who Attends?

Determine the size of your guest list by such considerations as: space, the kind of service you plan — buffet, dinner, dessert — and by whether you wish this to be an intimate gathering or a large, informal party. Approximately 15 people is a reasonable limit for the number of guests invited to a home shower.

If you are planning the shower personally, invite the guests of the bride-to-be-only. Don't ask friends of your own unless they know the girl who is being honored.

Members of both families, wedding attendants, and close friends are invited to showers. The event is rarely a surprise (as was formerly common), and the wise hostess will discuss the guest list with the bride. By doing so, the bride who will be given several showers can divide her friends so that no one goes to too many showers or purchases an inordinate number of gifts.

The mother of the bride and, if she is nearby, the mother of the groom are usually included as guests of honor, and are usually not expected to bring a gift. Other older people may be included too: relatives or family friends are usually happy to be a part of the festivities.

The majority of showers are given in the daytime, with the guest list composed of women. There is, however, an increasing trend toward mixed showers, held in the evening or on weekends, to which couples are invited. This type of shower, however, must be restricted to gifts and themes appropriate for both bride and groom. If you want to give a mixed shower built around a meal, it may be either a brunch or a dinner. An informal mixed shower might be a dessert-and-coffee party or a barbecue supper. When a shower is given by a fellow worker or member of a club, it is acceptable to invite co-workers or club members only.

There is no age limit to consider when inviting shower guests. Any person who is a friend of the bride-to-be may be invited. In the case of more intimate friends, however, it is customary to invite the mother of the bride and the groom's mothers, as well as their grand-mothers and sisters. Personal choices and general circumstances will aid the hostess in deciding for herself what is best.

Invitations

Invitations should usually be sent about two weeks before the date of the event, but this need not be strictly followed if circumstances make it necessary, as they frequently do, to give the guests shorter notice. During the holiday seasons, it is advisable to send invitations three weeks in advance if possible. An R.S.V.P. on a written invitation will serve as a reminder to your guests, and as a final guest list check for you.

Specify on the invitation the kind of shower being given so that your guests may come prepared. Personal notes may be written on paper or correspondence cards, or novelty shower invitations in keeping with your party theme may be purchased for the occasion. Since showers are informal affairs, engraved invitations are unnecessary. If you have artistic talent, you may want to make your own invitations. Of course, if the shower is to be a very small, informal one, you may telephone the invitations.

Always include all data in the invitation: date and time, the kind of occasion, and the purpose, and the place. Be sure to give address and directions for first-time guests coming to your home.

Menu

Decide what your menu will be, and also the quantities you will need for the number of guests you plan to invite. Consider, with your theme and menu in mind, what table service and accessories you will use. Refreshments at a shower naturally vary depending upon the time of day when it is held.

The kind of party you plan to have will determine your menu. Most of the theme showers discussed in this book require only light refreshments (dessert and beverage). Parties such as the ones discussed in chapter 4 obviously require more attention to the menu. When planning your menu, take your guests' special needs, if any, into consideration: diabetics and vegetarians both require special planning, and it is the responsibility of the bride to make the shower hostess aware of these special concerns.

There is no specific time for serving refreshments at a shower, but in most cases the hostess will probably prefer to serve them as the last part of the program. The advantage of this arrangement is that it brings the party to a close on a warm, congenial note, with the guests gradually departing, rather than ending the shower abruptly with the unwrapping of the last gift or the completion of the last game. It is again emphasized, however, that this is entirely a matter for the hostess to decide.

Decorations

The decorations for a shower may be simple or elaborate, depending upon the tastes of the hostess. A number of suggestions for decorations appropriate to specific showers are given in chapter 5, together with various ways to present the gifts.

Balloons, crepe paper streamers, paper ribbons, fresh flowers and leaves are often used as decorations. But here is a point where your imagination can really take over! Party props are great fun to use, and add immeasurably to party atmosphere. Flags, pictures, pennants, antiques, hobby and sports equipment, models, even children's toys may be used to create an imaginative setting.

Entertainment

The wise hostess is always prepared with a plan for a few games or activities, game props, and prizes. Some occasions are more appropriate for games than others. Many times an icebreaker activity and/or quiz is sufficient, and even these may be unnecessary. Some parties are so dominated by a steady stream of good conversation that games could spoil the fun. Be prepared with a few games, just in case — or just for fun. Adapt any of the old favorites to your party theme by changing game name and props to fit. Prizes are optional, but if they are used they should not be expensive, and should be prettily wrapped. In many regions of the country, it is customary for prizes received by guests at a bridal shower to be presented to the bride.

Tips for the Hostess

The more tasks you can take care of well in advance of the party, the more relaxed and composed you will be during the event. Several days before the party, check this list to see which pre-party steps apply to your entertaining plans, then do them!

- Arrange your schedule so that all housecleaning chores are completed well ahead of time, and your rooms look just the way you want them to look the day before the party.

- Write out your menu. Plan dishes that can be prepared in advance. Be sure your menu provides contrast in flavor, color, and texture. Check each recipe to make sure you have every ingredient. Avoid experimenting with a new recipe at a party, and try never to shop for essentials on the day of the event!

- Using your menu as a guide, take inventory of everything you will need for serving. Wash or polish your large serving pieces ahead of time.

- Take down your glasses and make sure there are enough — hopefully you will have extras if the party will be large. Check your silver to determine if it needs polishing.

- Inspect your china — plates, cups, saucers, platters — for chips. If you are planning a sit-down dinner, it's nice to have all the china match, but you can still have a lovely table by using two patterns and making every other place setting different. If you are serving buffet style, you can mix patterns in crystal and linen as well as china.

- Select the containers you will need for the flower or fruit arrangements you plan to use. You might want to take your favorite vase or bowl to the florist for a customized arrangement.

- Check your party linens for dust streaks or wrinkles. If cloths or place mats need pressing, do it in advance and put the linens on the table immediately.

- Be sure that you have plenty of hangers for guests' coats, and that your powder room has adequate soap and tissue.

- Decide what you will wear, and be sure it is cleaned and pressed.

- Freeze a good supply of ice cubes several days in advance, and store them in plastic bags.

- Place several ash trays in convenient locations if you have guests who smoke.

- From your party plan, make a master shopping list — for supermarket, stationers, florist, etc. Once your invitations are out, your party is underway; nothing remains but to work your plan.

- Use a guest book to keep a permanent record of all your parties so that the signatures in it will provide memories of the event in the years following. Guest books can be purchased at your local stationers or book store, or you may use an attractively-bound loose-leaf notebook.
- Place card holders made of china or silver add a lovely decorative touch to your table. Use matching holders, or put a different one at each place. The hostess can seat guests as she desires; thus, a good listener might be seated next to an avid conversationalist, etc.
- Provide a trash bag, scissors, and tape for the honoree to use when opening gifts. Arrange for someone to record the gifts, and be sure to have pen and paper handy.

Gifts for the Bride

Be discriminating in your selection of gifts for the guest of honor. In choosing a gift for any shower, it is always important to be very sure that the choice is the type and color that the guest of honor would select for *herself*, even though it may be something very different from what you would select for yourself. People's tastes vary widely, and no gift should be selected without keeping that in mind. Such thoughtfulness will be deeply appreciated by the bride-to-be.

The type of gift you select will partly be determined by the theme of the shower (see chapter 3), but often the choice of gift is left to the guest (see chapter 7). In years past, many shower gifts were hand-made items, and even today some people prefer to present a hand-made gift to the bride-to-be. However, most people do not have the time to devote to such projects.

Wedding presents are usually sent from the shop where they are purchased, but shower gifts are generally brought by the guests and presented personally upon arrival. If a friend cannot accept, she is not obligated to send a gift, but since a shower guest is generally a close friend or family member, she will undoubtedly want to do so. She sends the gift to the hostess' house ahead of time, so that it may be opened with the other presents.

Frequently the packages are taken at the door by the hostess and placed with the others. If the hostess is planning a special arrangement or presentation, she may ask the guests to bring their presents to her home a day or two ahead of time. She then adds outer wrappings to achieve the effect she desires. Gift cards should always be enclosed.

Note to the Guest

Just as the hostess and the bride have certain duties, so also are the guests expected to fulfill certain obligations. Upon receiving a shower invitation, do not delay too long in accepting or declining it. If it is necessary for you to decline the invitation, be sure to explain why. Only an emergency should prevent you from attending a shower if you have already accepted the invitation. When you are invited to a shower and you accept the invitation, you automatically agree to bring a gift. The gift you select should be useful, and not necessarily expensive. The thought or effort brings value to the gift, not the cost. Buying a shower gift does not excuse you from giving a wedding present if you have also received a wedding invitation.

In planning your time of arrival, always strive to arrive either exactly on time or slightly late. *Never* arrive early (unless you are co-hosting the party), as this will certainly cause problems for the hostess. Try to park your car in a way that does not block the drive for the other guests or the street for the neighbors. Also, don't offer to assist the hostess unless you are specifically asked to do so: unwanted "help" will only frustrate the hostess, and may even be offensive. Confine yourself to the party rooms, and stay out of the kitchen!

Strive to be an interesting conversationalist as well as a good listener. You will undoubtedly enjoy the party more if you are fresh and rested, so try to arrange your schedule in a way that will permit you to be at your best during the shower. Also, do not overstay your welcome: if the party is still going when the scheduled departure time arrives, feel free to excuse yourself — your hostess will be grateful. Say good-bye and thank you sincerely and briefly as you depart — try not to block the exit with an extended post-party conversation in the doorway. Do not call out final farewells from the drive or the street. Be sure to telephone the hostess a day or two after the party to express your appreciation.

Note to the Bride

The guest of honor should be considerate and helpful to the hostess in any way she can ahead of time, and should arrive about half an hour before the shower begins in order to assist in greeting and introducing the guests to one another.

Everyone realizes that an engaged girl is very busy making plans and preparations for her wedding, but this should not prevent her from writing thank-you notes for her shower gifts. These notes are usually short, simply mentioning the gift received and expressing thanks in a sincere manner. Don't forget to write a special thank you to each shower hostess also.

2

Themes

A bridal shower gives the bride's friends a chance to share in the festivities. The most important step in deciding which type of shower to give is to use your imagination! Because each shower is as unique as the person it honors, the wise hostess will choose the type of shower most appropriate under the circumstances. The following descriptions of different types of showers indicate the range of possibilities available to the shower hostess, but this should not prevent her from creating new shower themes or from modifying and combining these suggested themes to suit her own needs.

Kitchen Shower

Kitchen showers are always popular. Few rooms in the house require such a large variety of utensils and gadgets, and few gifts are as useful as those that equip the kitchen. Serve informally from your kitchen table. Use a red-and-white or blue-and-white checked tablecloth. Create a centerpiece of long-handled wooden spoons, wire whisks, spatulas, and other kitchen/pantry implements, or use an arrangement of fresh flowers in a copper teapot. Fruits and vegetables also make an appropriate centerpiece.

Linen Shower

Linen showers feature towels, washcloths, bath mats, shower curtains, bathroom scales, bedspreads, tablecloths, napkins, pillow cases, and sheets — anything found in a linen closet. Neutral colors are a "safe" choice if the bride has not yet worked out a color scheme for her linens.

In a shower of this type, the hostess should provide guests with bed size and color(s) in bedroom and bathroom. Because linens are costly, this type of shower is a good choice for the hostess and is always appreciated by brides.

Gifts may be presented in a wicker clothes basket decorated with crepe paper or ribbons. A set of sheets in the bride's color can be used as a tablecloth if desired. If you are giving an all-white linen shower, use a white tablecloth and a centerpiece of chrysanthemums, carnations, and daisies arranged in a white bowl.

Lingerie Shower

Lingerie showers, obviously for women only, should include only the bride's *close* friends and family members. The bride's sizes and color preferences should be included with the invitations. Gowns, robes, slips, hosiery, lingerie cases, and sachets are all appropriate gifts for a lingerie shower. Any item of lingerie is acceptable, and occasionally the guests pool their resources to purchase the bridal nightgown and robe.

The table decorations should be pink, peach, yellow, or pale blue to carry out the lingerie idea. For a centerpiece, use a crystal bowl of pastel-colored flowers placed on a mirror — and if the mirror is large enough, scatter some blossoms around the crystal bowl. Use a small chest of drawers for presenting the gifts. Tie ribbon bows to the handles and pile gifts on top and in the half-open drawers.

Recipe Shower

Guests bring their favorite recipes to help the bride with future cooking. These may be signed, filed, and presented to the honoree in a file box. There are four variations on this theme:

- Guests may bring their favorite recipe and the ingredients for making it.
- Guests may bring their favorite recipe and the utensil(s) in which to cook it.
- Guests may bring their favorite recipe as well as the ingredients and utensil(s) needed to prepare it.
- Guests may bring their favorite recipe as well as a finished sample of it already cooked. When this idea is used, the hostess should plan the menu so that each guest brings an item for a different course of the meal. Because the meat dish is usually the most expensive recipe, the hostess should prepare this herself.

This kind of shower is not limited to those who bring food and recipes. Other persons can be invited to share the meal who will bring gifts of their own choosing. Since the food provided on these occasions is often "extra-special," some hostesses prefer to give the shower as a buffet supper and invite the men as well as the women. Friends of the couple's parents will surely have numerous good recipe ideas, and it is appropriate to invite them also to a shower of this type.

Spice Shower

Guests contribute toward a spice cabinet for the couple, and each brings a different spice to fill it, as well as recipes featuring different spices. The hostess should specify which spice each guest should bring to avoid duplication. Other items appropriate for a spice shower are a spice chart and small pots of seeds for starting an indoor herb garden. A spice rack would make an appropriate hostess gift.

Gadget Shower

Guests bring the one household item they would most hate to lose! Pastry brush, carrot peeler, nut cracker, ice cream scoop — the list of household gadgets is endless. Any nice small gift is appropriate. It may be necessary for the hostess to coordinate the gifts in order to avoid duplication.

Groom's Shower

Although one usually thinks of wedding showers as occasions held in honor of the bride, increasingly showers are being held in honor of the groom as well as (or in addition to) the bride-to-be. Groom showers are hosted and attended exclusively by males.

The groom's shower is usually hosted by a member of the wedding party or a close personal friend. These parties tend to be very informal, and a cookout or patio party is usually a good idea, weather permitting. If held indoors, it can be a pizza party or a self-service sandwich bar.

In choosing a gift for the groom, give preference to lawn and household tools, outdoor cooking items, sports equipment, and automobile-related garage items.

Christmas Shower

Gifts for this shower would be Christmas tree ornaments and other items related to the holiday season. Packages should be wrapped in Christmas paper. Although certainly an excellent idea for the holiday season, it is appropriate to hold this shower at any time during the year using the Christmas theme for decorations and refreshments.

Miscellaneous

At a miscellaneous shower, guests bring something for any room in the house or a personal item for the bride. This is usually the type of shower the bride has if only one shower is given.

Pantry Shower

The idea of a pantry shower is, of course, to give the bride-to-be as many items of food for the pantry as possible. Since shelf paper is a pantry necessity, the hostess should either provide it herself or arrange for a guest to do so. Jams and jellies, relishes and spices, herbs, canned goods, tea, coffee, and gourmet specialties are all appropriate. Some hostesses ask their guests to bring staple foods such as corn starch, flour, corn meal, salt, pepper, sugar, and other foods that every newly-married couple needs.

This shower idea is a carry-over from the old New England custom of "pounding" newlyweds — each guest brought a "pound" of something for the pantry. This shower is especially appropriate for a student couple.

Personal Shower

This kind of shower is usally given by the bride's close friends, who know her sizes and preferences. Appropriate gifts are: lingerie, gloves, hosiery, costume jewelry, perfume, decorative boxes, scented bubble bath, dusting powder, soap and soap dishes, brushes and combs, manicure accessories, cosmetics, stationery — anything used exclusively by the bride herself. Decorate a large circular hat box in which to present the gifts.

Bride and Groom Shower

Several couples may enjoy hosting a bride-and-groom shower. Such showers are growing more and more popular in every community. All members of the wedding party would be invited to a couples shower. Any type of party may be planned — informal cookout, brunch, or buffet supper — with the groom and his friends present to share in the fun.

Suggested themes for a couple's shower are: kitchen, household accessory, or paper. Another idea is a western barbecue (decorate with red bandanas and western gear to create an "old west" atmosphere). Sometimes at a party of this type the group will present one large gift such as the entire set of casual dinnerware.

It is appropriate to hold a bride-and-groom shower either before or after the wedding.

Round-the-Clock Shower

A round-the-clock shower means that a certain hour of the day is written on each guest's invitation. She brings a gift appropriate to that hour: for example, a set of juice glasses or coffee mugs for 7:00 a.m., salad plates or placemats for 1:00 p.m., teacups and saucers for mid-afternoon, steak knives for 6:00 p.m., and bed linens or a lamp for evening. Guests are asked to mark their packages with the time of day for which they are intended. A clock, of course, is the perfect hostess gift. For a centerpiece, use a collection of timepieces including everything from egg timers to antique clocks.

Idea Shower

This shower calls for the guests to give their knowledge and experience rather than monetary gifts. The hostess asks each guest to help compile an "Ideas for the Bride" book to present to the guest of honor at the party.

The hostess includes four 3×5 cards with each invitation (so that the guests can list their favorite helpful hints for shopping, cooking, cleaning, and decorating) and provides a small, attractive binder for the cards. This is nice for a coffee, luncheon, or brunch.

Gourmet Shower

At this type of shower, the guests bring gifts of special jam, jelly, smoked oysters, imported cheese, wild rice, caviar, kippered herring, imported candies, fine tea and coffee, pickles and relishes, dried fruit and nuts, and any other food items which appeal to the discriminating palate. Cookbooks specializing in the preparation of gourmet foods are another appropriate gift idea.

Money Shower

The gifts for this shower are to be money, and may be either coins or currency, in various denominations. They should be displayed attractively in a decorative glass container, in a hand-painted piggy bank, or on a "money tree." To make a "money tree," spray a tree branch white, silver, or gold and anchor it in a pretty container. Tie ribbons to the branches to hold the gifts. Include small envelopes in colors to carry out your theme in the invitations. Guests put their contributions inside and write their name and a message on the outside, if desired. The hostess may want gifts sent or brought in advance so the tree will already be prepared when the bride arrives. At this shower, the honoree does not open the gifts. Instead, she takes the "tree" (or other container) with her. A group card or guest book signed by each guest may be presented to the honoree at the party.

Garden Shower

This shower should be given for those who are fond of green plants and gardening, and who intend to have a flower garden and/or vegetable garden. Usually the emphasis is placed upon flowers. Seeds, bulbs, and plants are wonderful gifts that provide lasting beauty for the lucky couple to whom they are given. The standard flowers can be given, as well as other less common varieties. For an apartment-dweller, these may need to be items for a window-box or terrace.

The hostess can consult with friends who are enthusiastic gardeners and get their ideas about the most interesting and unusual kinds of flowers and plants. The best place to hold a garden shower is in your own garden. Borrow garden chairs and umbrellas from your friends, if necessary: these will add to the attractiveness of the setting. Japanese lanterns can be hung on trees to create a festive decor. A large multi-colored garden hat holding a container filled with seasonal fresh flowers makes an attractive centerpiece. Use basket trays and serve refreshments informally.

As invitations, use cards decorated with colored illustrations of gardens. Some of these are very attractive and are available at most stationery stores. These can also be used as enclosure cards, attached to each gift bearing the guest's name. A possible hostess gift could be a lightweight wheelbarrow in which the other gifts can be piled for presentation to the guest(s) of honor.

Happy Hearts Shower

The heart theme is always a most appropriate one for a bridal shower. As far as the gifts are concerned, this may be any kind of shower at all, but the decorations and entertainment will create a romantic atmosphere that will make a "happy hearts" shower stand out from the usual round of bridal parties. A shower of this kind is particularly appropriate for a party given in February, the month that contains Valentine's Day. However, it need not be restricted to that time of year and is appropriate in any month since its theme is the perennial one of romance.

Valentines would make good invitations for this party. Note paper decorated with small red paper hearts is a good alternative.

In decorating, any arrangement of pink, white, and red flowers is appropriate as a centerpiece, as are tall red or white candles. Use a delicate lace tablecloth, and serve various heart-shaped foods. Cut your favorite sugar cookies into heart shapes, and decorate with red decorator sugar. Serve heart-shaped sandwiches for a festive tea or luncheon, and use heart-shaped molds for aspic or red molded fruit salads. Fill heart meringues with strawberries and ice cream, or serve Valentine heart pie or cake for dessert. Anything red or pink or heart-shaped will help carry out this theme. Give small candy holders filled with tiny red cinnamon hearts as party favors.

This shower could be a mixed party to which the friends of both the engaged girl and her fiancé are invited.

All-Year-Round Shower

This is a good "different" kind of shower that is always well-received when it is given. The idea is to give the bride-to-be gifts that are suitable and usable throughout the entire year. The hostess invites eleven of the engaged girl's friends to the party and assigns each a different month from which to choose a gift. The hostess herself makes the twelfth person, and she also selects a month for which to bring a suitable gift.

When the gifts are presented, the bride may wish to try to guess which gift represents each month.

Suggested gifts include:

- *January* — calendars of various kinds; personal diary; books of all kinds for reading during bad weather; knitting/needlework supplies; items for the medicine chest and first-aid kit
- *February* - current books on American history during the lifetimes of Washington and/or Lincoln; foods containing cherries; items related to Valentine's Day (perhaps a heart-shaped cake pan)
- *March* — a scarf for protection against March winds; something green to commemorate St. Patrick's Day (ashtrays, vases, pottery items, dish towels, placemats and napkins)
- *April* — something for April showers, such as an umbrella, raincoat, or rain hat; ceramic, glass, or wooden eggs to be used in an Easter centerpiece
- *May* — a bowl or vase in which to arrange fresh flowers; a silk flower arrangement
- *June* — a croquet set or badminton set for sunny summer days; lap trays and lawn chairs to use outdoors in hot weather
- *July* — a set of iced tea glasses and/or a large serving tray; a brightly-colored lawn umbrella; red-white-and-blue items for the Fourth of July
- *August* - travel guide books; a set of beach towels; suntan oil; picnic basket; portable cooler
- *September* — stadium blanket for football games; items displaying the couple's college emblem(s); an arrangement of dried flowers
- *October* — gifts suggesting Halloween, such as a ceramic pumpkin for a table decoration; orange candles; large fireplace matches
- *November* — gifts of food such as plum pudding or mincemeat are especially representative of the Thanksgiving month; a carving set; china turkey platter
- *December* — something suggesting Christmas; red and green candles; special recipes and food for the Holiday season; Christmas tree ornaments; a Christmas apron; a snow shovel

Book Shower

Brides are very seldom given books at their bridal showers or as wedding presents, yet a book shower is one of the best of all possible types. It usually takes time for a newly-married couple to accumulate an interesting collection of books, but a good book shower can get them started and can give them possessions they will treasure for many years. The books brought as gifts may be new releases or old favorites, and may be hardback or paperback editions. Paperbacks now include many classics and other quality reading material. Anthologies, subscriptions, book club memberships, bookends, and bookmarks all make excellent gifts. There are books every household needs: a Bible, cookbooks, first-aid manual, devotional books, a dictionary, classic fiction, and household do-it-yourself manuals.

Decorate with book jackets. Attractive promotional posters and displays may be available free from chain book stores, and these make interesting and different decorations.

There are numerous times before, during, and after the wedding when "how-to" wedding-related books (such as this one) are quite useful. Especially recommended as shower gift books are *After You've Said I Do* by Hardy Denham (JMP, $6.95) and *Financial Planning For Newlyweds* by Michael Speer (JMP, $6.95)

Basket Shower

This imaginative shower is intended for a girl who has a large number of friends and who is certain to receive numerous "normal" gifts at one or another of the usual, conventional showers.

The gifts at a basket shower consist of all the different kinds of pretty or useful baskets that the guests can find. These include: wastebaskets of several kinds, a sewing basket, and a towel basket for the bathroom. Other choices are garden baskets, picnic hampers, small decorated baskets for candy and nuts, and flower containers.

All these different baskets can be given to the honored guest in still another kind of useful basket. This may be either a wood basket for the fireplace or a large clothes hamper. The hostess will determine whether or not the basket should be full: for example, a sewing basket could contain a complete sewing kit. For full baskets, here is a list of ideas:

- *Arts and Crafts* — contains needlepoint/knitting items and instruction books.

- *Bathroom* — use a wastebasket filled with soaps and powders or guest towels.
- *Beverage* — filled with numerous juices and drink mixes.
- *Bottle* — contains ketchup, mustard, and other condiments. May also contain perfumes and colognes.
- *Brush* — filled with brushes of all kinds.
- *Cleaning* — filled with household cleaning items.
- *Convenience* — contains foods which require little or no preparation time and little or no cooking. Packaged dressings, sauces, snacks, cake mixes, and ready-to-eat foods in general are a few such items.
- *Glassware* — contains a nice set of tumblers.
- *Gourmet Items* — contains fine jams, jellies, and "special foods" such as caviar.
- *Green Thumb* — filled with seeds, plants, cuttings, and fertilizer.
- *Grocery* — filled with canned goods.
- *Kitchen Gadgets* — fill this with "little things" that are easy to overlook: measuring spoons, can or bottle opener, wire whisk, pastry brush, carrot peeler, etc.
- *Paper* — contains towels, facial tissue, and stationery.
- *Spice* — includes a variety of spices.

Picnic Shower

The object of this shower is to provide the engaged couple with useful items for picnics or outdoor parties. Gift items include a portable grill, cooking forks and knives, a picnic basket, tablecloths for outdoor use, plates, napkins, and cups, an ice bucket, and thermos bottle.

The party could be held outdoors, possibly in a park if the weather permits and a good location is convenient. Otherwise, it may be a buffet party held indoors.

Travel Shower

This shower is intended to provide the engaged girl with items she will need for traveling, both on her honeymoon and on subsequent trips. Gifts include luggage, travel clock, lingerie holders, shoe bags, small sewing kit, folding umbrella, steamer, cosmetic bag, travel guides, note paper, pen, and stamps. These items are frequently overlooked when a shower is given, and while useful for traveling they can also be used in the bride's home.

Decorate with travel posters; for example, a Hawaiian theme might feature posters of Hawaii, and each guest would receive a lei. Use luggage tags for place cards, and present the gifts in and around an open piece of luggage.

Paper Gift Shower

Many very useful items needed by a newly-married couple are made of paper, and a paper gift shower will help to give them some of these articles as well as give the guests a different kind of party. Gifts to bring to a shower of this kind include: writing paper and envelopes, calendars, playing cards, memo pads and notebooks, paper money, desk blotters, monogrammed napkins, coasters, towels and facial tissues. Magazine subscriptions are appropriate and are often welcome. Paper flowers, place mats, and book matches are other gift ideas. So many useful things are made of paper that it is not hard to find excellent paper gifts — use your imagination and creativity.

In presenting the gifts, arrange them on a table covered with a paper tablecloth and use a flower container filled with paper flowers as a centerpiece. Serve using paper plates and cups if the event is informal.

Glass and Plastics Shower

Gifts for a glass and plastics shower include a great many things that are invaluable to a new bride. Sometimes the guests purchase a complete set of glassware together, but usually the gifts consist of such things as: salt and pepper shakers, salad or dessert plates, large and small vases, inexpensive glasses for outdoor use, paperweights, casserole dishes, and ashtrays. Drinking glasses and goblets are the glass articles that one ordinarily thinks of first, and they are among the most appropriate.

Decorate the party rooms with crystal bowls of flowers. In displaying the gifts, place them in front of a large mirror where they can be reflected. Place glass Christmas balls at strategic locations to add to the colorfulness of the display. If available, use glass plates for serving.

Ice Cream Shower

Naturally, the theme of this party is ice cream! An ice cream freezer (from either the hostess or the group) makes a perfect gift for newlyweds, and so do gift certificates to a favorite ice cream parlor. Guests may want to provide their favorite ice cream recipes, which can be presented to the bride after gifts are opened. For refreshments, homemade ice cream is certainly the best idea.

Emergency Shelf Shower

Items needed during various kinds of emergencies (whether social emergencies or life-threatening ones) are the focus of this party. Guests may bring a recipe for a favorite dish and the ingredients to make it, so that the bride can keep them on an "emergency shelf" for unexpected guests. Other "emergency gifts" are candles, flashlights and batteries for power failures, matches, non-electric can opener, first-aid kit, "emergency foods" with a long shelf life (such as powdered milk and ready-to-eat canned items).

Painting Party

Often an engaged couple will want to give their new home a completely different color scheme. In this case, a painting party provides a way to have the new home painted with a minimum of trouble and expense, while friends have fun doing it.

The hostess must know ahead of time which colors will be needed. Her next job is to secure the equipment needed — paints, a large number of brushes in a variety of sizes, thinner, paint sticks, cloths, brush cleaner, and perhaps a ladder. Be sure to remind the guests to wear old clothes. Guests share the expense of the paint and brushes, and this together with their time is their gift to the new couple.

Plan this party far enough in advance so that the couple will have an opportunity to prepare their new home for painting — covering furniture, removing pictures from walls, etc. Listening to a radio or phonograph makes this work more enjoyable, and the hostess may want to make arrangements to have one at the party. The hostess may prefer not to prepare food in advance, electing instead to order pizza for delivery.

Bridge Shower

At dozens of showers given each year, the principal entertainment is playing bridge. This is certainly appropriate for friends who are members of bridge clubs and others who enjoy playing bridge. This type of shower would also make a nice couples party.

Breakfast Shower

It is optional whether or not this shower takes place during the breakfast hour, as well as whether or not breakfast foods are served at the party. This shower features utensils for making special items for breakfast, such as muffin tins, waffle iron, mixing bowls, mixing spoons, serving pitcher, cake and loaf pans, coffee pot or coffee maker, teapot, omelet pan, and toaster oven.

Keeping Clean Shower

The various gifts brought to this shower are sometimes overlooked at the usual bridal showers. When a keeping clean shower is given, the gifts consist of every imaginable cleaning aid and equipment — gloves for housework, silver polishing materials, soaps, dishcloths, dishtowels, feather duster, mops, brooms, dustpan, and various brushes. One of the countless centerpieces which can be made from such items is an arrangement of several feather dusters of different colors in a large vase or a similar container.

"Wish You Were Here" Shower

Occasionally the bride you want to honor lives in another town. When this happens, there are several ways to shower her from afar.

Decide on the kinds of gifts to send (unbreakable items preferred), and advise the guests of your plans. The hostess is responsible for planning and mailing the gifts: the "guests" at this kind of shower are responsible for bringing their gift to the hostess for mailing. Suggested gifts are recipes and the utensils used in their preparation. It is customary to place a telephone call to the bride during the event.

Do-It-Yourself

There are numerous other creative ways to plan parties and showers. You may want to use one or several of the following ideas in place of or in addition to the suggestions already listed. Some other shower themes are:

- Collector's shower (add to the bride's collection)
- Come-as-you-are shower
- Games shower
- Honeymoon shower
- Movie shower
- Music/record shower
- Soap shower
- Winter gifts shower

---3---

Party Ideas and Menus

The parties included in this chapter are ideal for entertaining and celebrating, and provide a chance for the new in-laws to meet or to become better acquainted as well as a get-together for the bridesmaids, and a party for both bride and groom. Gifts may be optional for these parties, depending on the hostess' wishes; however, a miscellaneous shower is an appropriate theme for any of the parties described in this chapter.

Fortunately, these parties, even when formal events, do not require that expensive dishes be served. In planning the menu, strive for variety and simplicity. Provide a pleasing array of colors in planning your food, as well as a tempting assortment of flavors and textures. Sometimes the simplest dishes are the most elegant, and are easiest on the host and hostess. If the bride or groom has a favorite dish, be sure to include it.

In decorating for these parties, you may wish to use the bride's chosen wedding colors in the table setting. Lots of pretty ribbon, lace, and flowers will help tie the theme together. Add a few simple touches to turn the event into something really special for the guests of honor.

Coffees

Coffees are a mid-morning gathering, usually held any time from 10:00 a.m. until noon. As a rule, they are simpler than brunch. The menu consists of coffee and another hot or cold beverage, depending on the season (usually hot chocolate or tea), coffee cake, sweet rolls on trays with lacy paper doilies, and sliced fresh fruit in a glass bowl or on a tray.

An informal coffee could be held in the garden in summer, using coordinated paper goods, or a formal setting in winter could be in

33

front of the fireplace using fine china.

Coffees are a way to mix business with pleasure, or sandwich an extra little party into busy days. They may be appropriate parties for co-workers to plan, to be held during coffee break at their place of work.

Appropriate Themes: Kitchen, Recipe, Idea, Spice, Gadget

* — denotes complete recipe in Chapter 6

SUGGESTED MENU:
FRESH STRAWBERRIES WITH SOUR CREAM SAUCE*
SAUSAGE BALLS*
CHEESE STRAWS*
WHOLE WHEAT COFFEE CAKE*
MINIATURE APPLESAUCE MUFFINS*
MOCHA PUNCH*
COFFEE

Brunches

Brunch, as the name implies, is a combination of breakfast and lunch, and may be served any time between 10:00 a.m. and 2:00 p.m. Probably the most popular brunches are co-ed affairs served late on Sunday morning.

A party at mid-day offers a change of pace from evening entertaining, and a brunch has charms quite different from those of a dinner party. Entertainment is optional at a brunch, and should occur after the meal. The location of the event will be determined by the hostess, and there are many excellent locations for this type of party. For example, a pool-side brunch for couples on a sunny weekend can be either casual or elegant, and provides a perfect setting. During cold weather, a fire-side brunch is charming and cozy.

Offer each guest a cup of coffee the moment he or she arrives. Buffet-style service at an informal brunch is most convenient, and a "forks only" type menu should be served, usually consisting of: fruit, cheese, sweet rolls and pastries, a casserole of eggs with bacon or sausage, coffee, and tea.

Appropriate Themes: Breakfast, Gourmet, Pantry, Emergency Shelf

SUGGESTED "PANCAKE PARTY" MENU:
CHILLED FRUIT JUICE
PLATTER OF HAM, BACON, AND SAUSAGE
PANCAKES*
WAFFLES*
A VARIETY OF TOPPINGS
COFFEE
MILK

Luncheons

Luncheons are a nice way to honor a bride and are a good party choice for a small group of close friends. They may be held in a private home, at a country club, or in the private dining room of a restaurant. Luncheons may be either sit-down or buffet-style. The menu usually consists of a salad and dainty sandwiches, beverage, and dessert. Keep the menu light, but do not forget to add your own "special touches" wherever possible. Provide table favors, perhaps a single flower at each plate. Be a bit adventurous: most women love trying something new.

If held at a restaurant, the honoree usually receives a gift from the hostess. A collective gift from the other friends is optional.

Appropriate Themes: Linen, Lingerie, Personal

SUGGESTED MENU:
CHICKEN SALAD IN CANTALOUPE RING*
MARINATED ASPARAGUS
ASSORTED RELISH TRAY
HEART-SHAPED SANDWICHES
STRAWBERRY PARFAIT*
TEA PUNCH*

Teas

Despite the fact that most people today lead casual lifestyles, some occasions seem to require a formal, fairly large daytime party. At these times, a tea is the ideal solution. Because of its unchanging traditions, this kind of party provides an ideal climate for mixing guests of all ages.

Teas are drop-in, come-and-go parties between certain hours (usually 2:00 - 6:00 p.m.). The table is set with an assortment of dainty sandwiches, cookies, petits fours, and candies. Even the most casual hostess should forego the convenience of instant foods and shortcuts, presenting instead an elegant menu.

Much less formal but still traditional is the intimate tea for a few friends. At such a get-together, just tea is served and the decorations are quite informal. This is also the perfect time for the true tea lover to offer her guests some of the more exotic varieties of tea.

For a gift tea, the miscellaneous theme is most appropriate.

SUGGESTED MENU FOR A LARGE TEA OR RECEPTION:

TEA SANDWICHES*
PETITS FOURS
WEDDING COOKIES*
TEA CAKES*
FRESH FRUIT
CHEESE BALL*
CRACKERS
PARTY CANDY*
NUTS
HOT SPICED TEA*
PUNCH*

SUGGESTED MENU FOR A SMALL TEA:

ASSORTED TEA SANDWICHES*
STRAWBERRY TARTS*
PARTY MINTS*
MIXED NUTS
HOT FRUITED TEA* OR TEA DELIGHT*

Dinners

Everybody loves a dinner party — it's such a friendly way to entertain and to be entertained. Good food and good conversation in a comfortable atmosphere naturally result in a good time for both guests and hostess. There is a large variety of types of dinners from which to choose — casual or elegant, small or large.

In addition to formal events, there are also all sorts of informal get-togethers that seem particularly suited to certain seasons, occasions, or groups of friends. For a pleasant change of pace or for entertaining many people at one time, buffet suppers are the perfect solution. Mix china, linens, and serving pieces; you won't disturb the decor. You can mix people more freely, too. It is certainly appropriate to invite guests of all ages.

Buffet service is the perfect answer for the novice or busy hostess, or for accommodating a large group. The arrangement of a buffet is a matter of both common sense and convenience. If the meal is to be served on a sideboard or table pushed against the wall, the arrangement described below is the most logical.

Begin at one end of the table with plates, then move on to the meat or main dish, vegetables, salad, breads, condiments, silver, and finally napkins. Guests should finish at the end of the table nearest the door in order to eliminate congestion. For a larger crowd, place the table in the center of the room and duplicate service on both sides so that two lines of guests may serve themselves at the same time.

If you are having a formal buffet where guests will be seated at your dining room table, set the table exactly as you would for a formal dinner. A card-table buffet operates in the same way, except that the dining room table is used as the buffet serving table. Card tables set up in the living room or on the patio have the silver, glasses, and napkins in place. Provide salt and pepper shakers for each table. Use miniature centerpieces to complement the main buffet table.

The most important consideration in buffet dining is the menu, for buffet service demands easy-to-eat "fork" foods. If you have enough of them, individual lap trays are an asset. Decorative casseroles and chafing dishes, handsome electrical appliances, colorful table accessories, and other serving aids simplify your entertaining and improve the appearance of your table settings. Your table will also reflect your hospitality if you use sparkling glass, silver, china, linens, and table decorations.

Buffet service is simple because guests serve themselves. However, the hostess usually serves water after the guests are seated and she also refills serving dishes as needed.

Just before the guests have finished, the hostess clears the buffet and arranges the dessert plates and silver on the table, or coffee and dessert may be served from a side table.

Other fun and easy ways to entertain informally are a progressive dinner, a spaghetti supper, a fondue party, or a Polynesian picnic.

Undoubtedly the most popular party for warm-weather entertaining is the one served in your own backyard. Whether you call it a barbecue supper, cookout, or patio party, the keynote of the occasion is informality. Guests and hosts alike may dress casually.

More often than not, the man of the house turns chef at such times and takes over the cooking of the meat on a grill. The hostess serves the remaining foods and later serves a dessert that she has prepared in advance. Paper plates and napkins are sometimes used, which not only sets the informal tone of the occasion but also facilitates clean-up afterward.

The menu listed below is for an informal dinner with a Mexican theme. A related idea for decorating for a Mexican meal would be to use a large basket of Mexican paper flowers as a centerpiece.

Appropriate Themes: Pantry, Gourmet, Kitchen

SUGGESTED INFORMAL MEXICAN DINNER MENU:

MEXICAN CASSEROLE*
TAOS SALAD*
FRUIT AND CHEESE TRAY*
MAKE-YOUR-OWN-SUNDAE*

SUGGESTED BUFFET DINNER MENU:

MARINATED EYE OF THE ROUND*
WILD RICE CASSEROLE*
GREEN VEGETABLES WITH SAUCE*
TOMATO ASPIC IN HEART-SHAPED MOLDS
ROLLS
CHERRY TORTE*
TEA
COFFEE

Dessert Parties

A dessert-and-coffee party scheduled for some convenient time after dinner is a nice idea for any hostess, but is an especially attractive option for the girl with a job or for the young couple with a tiny kitchen. It's also ideal for week-night entertaining because such a party generally ends early and leaves the hostess with a minimum of clean-up.

The day before the party, prepare a spectacular dessert. On party night, all that remains is to put the finishing touches on your dessert and to make the coffee. Serve as soon as the guests arrive. Serving from a tea cart will lend a dramatic touch to the occasion: place the dessert, coffee, nuts, and mints of the top shelf, and cups, plates, napkins, and silver on the lower shelf.

Appropriate Themes: Happy Hearts, Bridge, Ice Cream, Money

SUGGESTED DESSERT MENU:

(any of the desserts listed in Chapter 6 are appropriate)
HEART MERINGUES*
MINTS*
NUTS
SPECIAL COFFEE*

Snack Parties

Snack parties are quite flexible in that they may be held almost anywhere and at almost any hour. They are among the easiest of parties to plan and host, but like all parties they must be well-planned in advance in order to succeed. Snacks are always served buffet-style: arrange all foods (including cake and coffee) on the buffet so that guests can serve themselves. For a very small party, snacks may be served from a tray on the living room coffee table (possibly in front of the fireplace), or on the patio. The hostess' main task at a snack party is to replenish the buffet as needed.

The menu consists of several finger foods selected with a view toward creating a pleasant diversity of colors, tastes, and textures. Balance crunchy items (such as raw vegetables or chips) with a creamy dip, or contrast ice-cold shrimp with sizzling meatballs. Pale cheeses balance nicely against dark, ripe olives in terms of color.

By assembling a large variety of snack foods, it is possible to offer a "snack smorgasbord" that takes the place of dinner. Such a meal might feature platters of ham and cheese, or a fondue. You may also wish to include a salad and/or soup. Whether you are serving just a few items or a large variety that takes the place of a meal, there are two general guidelines to remember: concentrate on "pick-up foods" and bite-size portions that can be handled with the fingers or speared with wooden picks; and emphasize spicy foods instead of sweet ones. Many of these snacks convert easily to a first course for a party dinner.

Appropriate Themes: Book, Paper Gift, Entertainment (Games, Music, Movies), Painting Party

SUGGESTED MENU:
TRAY OF THINLY-SLICED HAM, BEEF, AND CHEESE
SALMON BALL*
APPETIZER LOAF*
ARTICHOKE DIP*
RAW VEGETABLE TRAY
FRESH FRUIT TRAY*
ASSORTED BREADS AND CRACKERS
BEVERAGES OF YOUR CHOICE
BROWN SUGAR POUND CAKE*
COFFEE

4

Seasonal Ideas and Decorations

Decoration can add interest to a bridal shower and contribute significantly to making it a festive occasion. Usually it is best to choose a theme that you can carry out in decorations, centerpiece, menu, entertainment, and presentation of gifts. In any case, decorations should always coordinate with the theme of the shower. Most hostesses find that a few decorator touches add enormously to the festivities. The number of ways to decorate cleverly is endless! In party decorations, virtually anything goes, and bright, artful, amusing items are best. The following suggestions will spark your imagination.

Seasonal Ideas

• *January* — Hold an open house or a New Year's good luck party (perhaps an informal dinner). Use good luck symbols such as horseshoes, 4-leaf clovers, and wishbones in decorating.

• *February* — Valentine theme (see Chapter 2, "Happy Hearts Shower")

• *March* — Plan a St. Patrick's Day party. Carry out this theme by using green decorations and favors. Serve green-iced cakes or shamrock-shaped cookies. Any number of themes would be appropriate; perhaps a "Round-the-Clock Shower" or an "All-Year-Round Shower."

• *April* — Use the Easter theme featuring Easter bunnies, lilies, and eggs. An Easter brunch or "Basket Shower" is appropriate.

• *May* — Plan a "Garden Shower." Decorate with spring flowers and blossom branches, together with colored crepe paper streamers and May baskets containing bouquets or candy.

• *June* — The traditional month for weddings. This month is most appropriate for couple showers featuring brunches, informal dinners and snack parties.

- *July* — Independence Day theme; American flags and red-white-and-blue streamers can be used for decorations. Use a blue denim tablecloth with red-and-white bandanas as napkins and bread basket liner. Place serving dishes on aluminum foil stars. A "Paper Gift Shower" or a "Glass and Plastics Shower" would be seasonal.

- *August* — No holidays; a vacation month. An "Ice Cream Shower," a "Travel Shower," or a "Picnic Shower" would be most appropriate.

- *September* — Labor Day observed; A "Kitchen Shower," "Pantry Shower," or "Keeping Clean Shower" are most suitable.

- *October* — Decorate with a jack-o'-lantern centerpiece and other Halloween symbols, as well as corn stalks, autumn leaves, and orange-and-black confetti. Serve hot spiced cider and give corn candy favors. A "Book Shower" or a "Spice Shower" are appropriate.

- *November* — Thanksgiving observed; a buffet dinner/"Gourmet Shower" is appropriate. Refer to this chapter for decorating and centerpiece ideas.

- *December* — Plan a "Christmas Shower" or a "Money Shower." Presents can be grouped on or around the tree. Plan Christmas carols for entertainment and use traditional Christmas decor.

Use the following as general decorating ideas:

- Flowers
- Balloons
- Bride-and-groom figurines
- Wedding ring designs
- Wedding bells
- Lace fans
- Plants
- Blossoming fruit tree branches
- Fall leaves
- Large baskets filled with cornstalks, winter grasses, and Indian corn
- Festive Christmas runner: sew green ball fringe around the edge of a length of red-and-white-striped fabric and use on a red or white tablecloth

42

- Colored bells (5 or 6) tied onto the bread basket with a narrow ribbon (Christmas luncheon)
- Valentine's Day: use a lace tablecloth, lace place mats, or cut-work place mats
- Valentine's Day: cover the table with a red or pink cloth and use white lace place mats
- Valentine's Day: stitch red felt hearts on a pink runner and use on a plain white tablecloth
- Easter: use delicate Spring flowers everywhere. Green, yellow, and white are the traditionally popular Easter colors, but lavender and pink are also widely used.
- Make a "Holiday Tree" using medium-sized tree branches in an attractive container. Spray-paint them white or a metallic color (depending on your color scheme for the party). Fill the container with green paper "grass" at the base. A Holiday tree also makes a festive centerpiece for the table: use small branches in a vase or flower pot to create a table-sized tree.
  - Valentine's Day: Trim with red paper hearts of varying sizes, pink and red bows, and/or decorated heart-shaped cookies and candies. Accent with tiny artificial flowers.
  - St. Patrick's Day: Use green paper shamrocks of different sizes, green and white bows, and/or decorated cookies and candies. Accent with various good luck charms and tiny artificial flowers.
  - Easter: Decorate the tree with any combination of colored eggs, Easter cookies, novelty Easter candies, or artificial small Spring flowers.
- A miniature bridal bouquet/corsage of tiny flowers and leaves, framed with a paper doily and tied with narrow ribbon, makes an excellent place card and/or party favor.
- Use tiny baskets filled with Easter candy at each place setting as a place card and/or party favor
- Use a bright print tablecloth with coordinating napkins for a summer outdoor party
- Use a quilt as a tablecloth

Candles

Tall handsome candles are a must for a friendly, intimate atmosphere. Use candles lavishly:

- Place tall tapers or three-branch candelabras on the sideboard or mantle
- Place single candles as tiny centerpieces for card table service
- Place yellow beeswax candles in an arrangement of vegetables and straw flowers
- Arrange seasonal leaves, ferns, or evergreens around the base of a row of graduated candles
- Place a tall candle in slender candlestick, and place on table; stack apples around it in a circular pattern several rows high, and fill in with greenery (Christmas)
- Use a large, single red candle surrounded by holly on a red cloth runner (Christmas)

Use fruits in monochromatic combinations:
- Make a red arrangement with strawberries, apples, tomatoes, cranberries, red grapes, or plums, perhaps mixed with pieces of cranberry or Bavarian glass
- Arrange oranges, peaches, nectarines, and apricots in a brass bowl
- Combine avocados, artichokes, acorn squash, and cucumbers in a green basket with a bunch of green grapes tied to the handle

Use spray to enhance anything shapely:
- Frost fir branches with white
- Gild a pineapple
- Spray artichokes silver
- Put a sheen on dull vegetables or nuts with clear plastic spray

Use unusual containers and heirloom pieces:
- Apothecary jars
- Casseroles
- Copper and pewter pieces
- Soup tureen
- Stemmed goblets (for twin centerpieces, with a single flower floating in each)
- Tall pitcher
- Tea pot (porcelain, ceramic, or pottery)
- Umbrella stands

Centerpieces

The centerpiece may be tall and striking in appearance, but should not overwhelm your attractive party foods. Often the only centerpiece used is a fresh flower arrangement, but it is also appropriate to use a cake decorated with white or pastel icing placed on a footed cake stand. The gifts themselves, attractively arranged with garlands of flowers or piled in a pretty container (such as a colorful umbrella), may also provide the main table decoration.

Delightful arrangements may be made of:

- A pair of hurricane lamps filled with flowers, cherries, glass marbles, holly sprigs, or paper flowers
- An attractive tree limb sprayed white, gold, or any pastel color and secured in a silver or glass bowl, decorated with miniature wedding bells, hearts, flowers, or paper umbrellas
- Fruit piled on a cake stand
- Sweet rolls, doughnuts, croissants, and muffins piled in a basket surrounded by fresh leaves, holly, or flowers (coffee or brunch)
- Ivy twined around driftwood
- Small ceramic figures combined with a few flowers on a mirror base
- Yellow and white daisies and mums arranged with green grapes and leaves in a white compote
- A pineapple, bananas, pears, apples, lemons, and a variety of nuts sprayed gold and placed in a compote surrounded by greenery
- A doll's house encircled by fresh flowers from which ribbons run to each place setting
- A glass bowl filled with cat-tails, seed pods, and winter grasses
- Shiny fresh fruits and vegetables, gourds and/or ears of corn arranged in a pottery bowl
- Dark green acorn squash, amber winter onions, dried red peppers, and white or yellow daisies arranged in a low wooden bowl
- Graceful sprays of wheat combined with chrysanthemums in an antique container
- Red cabbage, acorn and yellow squash, white and yellow onions, pumpkin, eggplant, green peppers, apples, grapes, and oranges placed on a tray lined with autumn leaves and flanked by tall yellow candles in glass holders
- A hollowed-out pumpkin filled with vivid autumn flowers (use two pumpkins for a long table)
- A silver bowl filled with silver or blue ornaments
- A large milk glass bowl filled with white sprayed evergreen branches and trimmed with small white ornaments (Christmas)

• A silver bowl filled with silver balls and holly leaves (Christmas)

• Combine pieces of driftwood into an abstract tree shape and trim with strings of popcorn and cranberries, gingerbread men, and miniature candles (Christmas)

• Fill a basket or bowl with pastel-tinted eggs made of glass, ceramic, wood, or candy (Easter)

• Place a huge chocolate bunny in a bed of Easter "grass," and surround it with tinted eggs (Easter)

Christmas Tree Trims

• Hang artificial fruits and nuts on a white flocked tree; tie the fruits on with red velvet bows; fill in with red ball ornaments

• Make an old-fashioned tree with popcorn balls, candy canes, and strings of cranberries and popcorn

• Hang decorated Christmas cookies on the tree with ribbon

• Attach artificial red roses to the branches of your tree; use red or pink roses on a white tree, pale blue ones on a green tree

Decorating a Wreath

An inexpensive wreath, tastefully decorated, is both decorative and festive. Cover the wreath with ribbon that is appropriate for your color scheme and theme. Attach miniatures which express your shower theme. Complete with a bow. If desired, make additional bows from the excess ribbon to use on green plants, candles, or trays.

• For any bridal shower: use white ribbon, lace, wedding rings, flowers, wedding bells, etc.

• Kitchen shower: use miniature measuring spoons, cups, or any small kitchen device

• Spice shower: attach containers of spices with the same ribbon in which the wreath is wrapped

• Coffee: attach a miniature cup and saucer

• Easter: attach flowers and/or colored eggs

• Christmas:
  — Candy and cookie wreath; use bright ribbons to tie individually-wrapped cookies, candies and nuts to a wreath; add a large bow;

— Pine cones and leaves; add red ball ornaments to wreath for color;
— Wreath of roses; cover wreath with paper roses or other flowers; fill in with tiny ball ornaments

[For additional information on entertaining and decorating, see *It's Fun To Entertain* by Blackie Scott (Atlanta: Peachtree, 1983), $9.95]

Party Games

Although games are inappropriate for many of the parties in this book, it is likely that at some time every shower hostess will want or need to introduce games of one kind or another into the festivities. Whether as an icebreaker for new acquaintances or as a friendly competition, party games are an ideal, inexpensive way for your guests to enjoy themselves.

How Did They Meet?

A fun way to begin a shower is to have each married guest (including the guest of honor) describe how she and her husband first met. If the guests have amusing wedding stories about their own weddings, these can be included also.

Let's Get Acquainted

Ask each guest to write down their personal answers to the following list of favorites. When all 12 favorites have been answered, the bride-to-be then reads her answers to the group. The person with the most answers matching the bride's answers wins the game.

What is your favorite:

1. color _____

2. dessert _____

3. season _____

4. flower _____

5. song _____

6. beverage _____

7. holiday _____

8. performer _____

9. automobile _____

10. television program _____

11. flavor of ice cream _____

12. book _____

Meet the Bride

Provide the contestants with pencil and paper, and ask the bride to leave the room for 5-10 minutes until they have completed their answers. The person with the most correct answers wins. Some questions may be omitted if inappropriate.

1. What color shoes is she wearing? _____
2. Is her wedding diamond set in yellow or white gold? _____
3. What is the date of the wedding? _____
4. What is the bridegroom's name? _____
5. What colors has the bride selected for the wedding? _____
6. What color is she wearing? _____
7. How tall is she? _____
8. What color is her hair? _____
9. What is her fiancé's occupation? _____
10. Is she wearing a watch? _____
11. How much does she weigh? _____
12. What color is her slip? _____
13. How did the couple meet? _____
14. Where will they live? _____
15. What kind of car do they have? _____
16. What is the bride's favorite color? _____
17. What is her favorite flower? _____
18. What is her favorite sport? _____
19. Where is her favorite vacation spot? _____
20. What kind of music does she like best? _____
21. What was her favorite subject in school? _____
22. What is her favorite month of the year? _____
23. What is her favorite kind of food (Italian, Mexican, Chinese, etc.)? _____
24. What is her favorite leisure-time activity? _____
25. What is her favorite perfume? _____
26. What is her favorite song? _____
27. Which animal is her favorite pet? _____
28. Which flavor of ice cream does she like most? _____
29. Where was she born? _____
30. Where was her fiancé born? _____

Cake Contest

Use your imagination to answer the following questions using different kinds of cake.

What kind of cake would you serve to:

1. A thin person? _____

2. A cheater? _____

3. An unkind person? _____

4. A dull person? _____

5. One who likes vegetables? _____

6. A driver in slow traffic? _____

7. A lazy person? _____

8. A star gazer? _____

9. A gloomy person? _____

10. The yard man? _____

11. Your favorite person? _____

12. A crazy person? _____

13. A potter? _____

14. A baseball player? _____

15. Adam and Eve? _____

16. Astronauts in space? _____

17. A sourpuss? _____

18. A banker? _____

19. A fashion designer? _____

20. A painter? _____

Add Spice

Match the words and word fragments from the list below to complete the corresponding name of a spice.

ARD   ME   MON   GER   SAME   IT   MIN
RIKA   SE   LEAF   VES   POWDER   MEG
MARY   SEED   LIC   GANO   SPICE   SIL   GE
POWDER   SEASONING   PER   SEED   LL

1. must _____

2. di _____

3. all _____

4. rose _____

5. bay _____

6. nut _____

7. cu _____

8. poultry _____

9. ani _____

10. pap _____

11. sa _____

12. clo _____

13. curry _____

14. se _____

15. thy _____

16. poppy _____

17. gin _____

18. gar _____

19. cinna _____

20. ba _____

21. ore _____

22. chili _____

23. pep _____

24. caraway _____

25. sa _____

Wedding Anniversaries

Match the anniversary to the gift that commemorates it (list taken from *The Wedding Anniversary Idea Book* by Rayburn and Rose Ann Ray, JMP 1985).

_____ 1. First	(a) iron or candy	
_____ 2. Second	(b) tin, aluminum	
_____ 3. Third	(c) paper	
_____ 4. Fourth	(d) pearl	
_____ 5. Fifth	(e) crystal	
_____ 6. Sixth	(f) steel	
_____ 7. Seventh	(g) diamond	
_____ 8. Eighth	(h) gold	
_____ 9. Ninth	(i) lace	
_____ 10. Tenth	(j) silver	
_____ 11. Eleventh	(k) emerald	
_____ 12. Twelfth	(l) electrical appliances	
_____ 13. Thirteenth	(m) wood or clocks	
_____ 14. Fourteenth	(n) pottery or willow	
_____ 15. Fifteenth	(o) copper, bronze, brass, wool	
_____ 16. Twentieth	(p) cotton	
_____ 17. Twenty-fifth	(q) china	
_____ 18. Thirtieth	(r) ivory	
_____ 19. Thirty-fifth	(s) silk, linen	
_____ 20. Fortieth	(t) leather	
_____ 21. Forty-fifth	(u) ruby	
_____ 22. Fiftieth	(v) diamond	
_____ 23. Fifty-fifth	(w) jade, coral	
_____ 24. Sixtieth	(x) sapphire	
_____ 25. Seventy-fifth	(y) books, fruit, flowers	

Kitchen Activity

Choose the word from the list below which best completes the phrase about culinary activity. Allow 5-10 minutes to complete the list. The person with the largest number of correct answers wins.

PEEL   WHIP   MARINATE   SLICE   SCRAPE   ROAST
BEAT   BREW   TOSS   KNEAD   CRACK   SPRINKLE
SIFT   FROST   CORE   OPEN   FRY   TOAST   MOLD
SCRAMBLE   BASTE   WARM   SAUTÉ   CUT   BOIL   GREASE

1. _____ the pie

2. _____ the flour

3. _____ the salad

4. _____ the cake

5. _____ the roast

6. _____ the eggs

7. _____ the apples

8. _____ the bananas

9. _____ the cans

10. _____ the cream

11. _____ the rolls

12. _____ the onion

13. _____ the steaks

14. _____ the pans

15. _____ the cookies

16. _____ the water

17. _____ the batter

18. _____ the turkey

19. _____ the jello

20. _____ the dough

21. _____ the chicken

22. _____ the bread

23. _____ the salt

24. _____ the coffee

25. _____ the nuts

26. _____ the bowl

Monthly Flowers

Match the month on the left with its special flower on the right.

_____ 1. January   (a) Chrysanthemum

_____ 2. February   (b) Aster

_____ 3. March   (c) Gladiolus

_____ 4. April   (d) Larkspur

_____ 5. May   (e) Rose

_____ 6. June   (f) Holly

_____ 7. July   (g) Lily of the Valley

_____ 8. August   (h) Daisy

_____ 9. September   (i) Daffodil

_____ 10. October   (j) Violet

_____ 11. November   (k) Calendula

_____ 12. December   (l) Carnation

Culinary Unscramble

Unscramble these kitchen words in 10 minutes or less. The person with the most correct answers wins.

1. xmire _____
2. opoatt elpere _____
3. rbelnde _____
4. lirolgn npi _____
5. sparty ubsrh _____
6. oaedclrn _____
7. lirbroe _____
8. aictrnse _____
9. apynrt _____
10. atsualp _____
11. hsdewhiasr _____
12. rrtgoarfriee _____
13. fnike _____

14. acn eprneo _____
15. rasotre _____
16. ikoceo ajr _____
17. otvse _____
18. rfko _____
19. akce nap _____
20. tegarr _____
21. odof rpscrsooe _____
22. flawef niro _____
23. sliklet _____
24. greasmuni puc _____
25. doonew snoop _____

Proverbial Wisdom

Fill in the blanks to complete the following "tried and true" sayings. Finish as many as you can in 5 minutes, and the person with the most correct answers wins.

1. A stitch in time _____

2. Better late _____

3. Never put off until tomorrow _____

4. A watched pot _____

5. A bird in hand _____

6. What's good for the goose _____

7. There are two sides _____

8. The early bird catches _____

9. All's well _____

10. A penny saved _____

11. Absence makes _____

12. All's fair _____

13. Two can live _____

14. He who falls in love with himself _____

15. All the world _____

Gourmet Cooking

Ask each guest to try to unscramble the following list of words related to gourmet cooking. Allow 5-10 minutes to complete the list. The person with the most correct answers is the winner.

1. oprliabn _____

2. chbnla _____

3. mcera_____

4. vlodssei _____

5. lgzae _____

6. treag _____

7. denak_____

8. ataemnir _____

9. hoapc_____

10. sueta _____

11. phwi _____

12. rsmmei _____

13. drhse _____

14. cnmei_____

15. kpreoco_____

Answers

Cake Contest

1. Pound
2. Fudge
3. Devil's Food
4. Spice
5. Carrot
6. Jam
7. Sponge
8. Milky Way
9. Sunshine
10. Prune
11. Angel Food
12. Banana
13. Cup Cakes
14. Bundt
15. Apple
16. Upside-Down
17. Lemon
18. Gold
19. Chiffon
20. Rainbow

Add Spice

1. mustard
2. dill
3. allspice
4. rosemary
5. bay leaf
6. nutmeg
7. cumin
8. poultry seasoning
9. anise
10. paprika
11. sage
12. cloves
13. curry powder
14. sesame
15. thyme
16. poppy seed
17. ginger
18. garlic
19. cinnamon
20. basil
21. oregano
22. chili powder
23. pepper
24. caraway seed
25. salt

Wedding Anniversaries

1-C; 2-P; 3-T; 4-Y; 5-M; 6-A;
7-0; 8-L; 9-N; 10-B; 11-F; 12-S;
13-I; 14-R; 15-E; 16-Q; 17-J;
18-D; 19-W; 20-U; 21-X; 22-H;
23-K; 24-G; 25-V

Kitchen Activity

1. slice
2. sift
3. toss
4. frost
5. baste
6. scramble
7. core
8. peel
9. open
10. whip
11. warm
12. sauté
13. marinate
14. grease
15. cut
16. boil
17. beat
18. roast
19. mold
20. knead
21. fry
22. toast
23. sprinkle
24. brew
25. crack
26. scrape

Monthly Flowers

January-Carnation; February-Violet; March-Daffodil; April-Daisy; May-Lily of the Valley; June-Rose; July-Larkspur; August-Gladiolus; September-Aster; October-Calendula; November-Chrysanthemum; December-Holly

Culinary Unscramble

1. mixer
2. potato peeler
3. blender
4. rolling pin
5. pastry brush
6. colander
7. broiler
8. canister
9. pantry
10. spatula
11. dishwasher
12. refrigerator
13. knife
14. can opener
15. roaster
16. cookie jar
17. stove
18. fork
19. cake pan
20. grater
21. food processor
22. waffle iron
23. skillet
24. measuring cup
25. wooden spoon

Gourmet Cooking
1. panbroil
2. blanch
3. cream
4. dissolve
5. glaze
6. grate
7. knead
8. marinate
9. poach
10. sauté
11. whip
12. simmer
13. shred
14. mince
15. precook

Proverbial Wisdom
1. A stitch in time saves nine.
2. Better late than never.
3. Never put off until tomorrow what you can do today.
4. A watched pot never boils.
5. A bird in hand is worth two in the bush.
6. What's good for the goose is good for the gander.
7. There are two sides to every question.
8. The early bird catches the worm.
9. All's well that ends well.
10. A penny saved is a penny earned.
11. Absence makes the heart grow fonder.
12. All's fair in love and war.
13. Two can live as cheaply as one.
14. He who falls in love with himself will have no rivals.
15. All the world loves a lover.

——— 6 ———

Recipes

This chapter consists exclusively of various kinds of recipes appropriate for showers. Most of them are included in suggested menus in chapter 3 (marked there with *), but additional recipes have been included as well so that the creative hostess can plan according to her personal tastes and needs.

APPETIZERS, SNACKS, AND SANDWICHES

Sausage Balls

3 cups biscuit mix
1 pound hot sausage at room temperature

2 cups grated cheddar cheese
6 - 8 tablespoons water

Combine biscuit mix, sausage, and cheese, and blend well. Add enough water to moisten. Make into one-inch balls and place on cookie sheet. Bake in 400 degree oven about 15 minutes or until brown. Yield: 60-70.

To freeze: place on cookie sheet in freezer until firm, then store in heavy plastic bag.

Cheese Straws

½ pound grated sharp cheddar cheese
1 stick soft butter

¼ teaspoon salt
⅛ teaspoon cayenne pepper
1½ cups flour

Cream butter and add cheese, then blend thoroughly. Add flour slowly. Add seasoning. Separate and form into rolls. Wrap in waxed paper and place in refrigerator. When thoroughly chilled, slice and place on cookie sheet. Bake at 425 degrees for about 20 minutes or until golden brown. Yield: about 70.

These may be frozen before baking. Ground dates, poppy seeds, crisp cooked bacon, or ripe olives may be added.

Cheese Ball

1 pound grated cheddar cheese
1 cup chopped walnuts
2 3-ounce packages softened
   cream cheese

1 tbsp. Worcestershire sauce
¼ teaspoon garlic powder
2 tbsp. instant minced onion
1 tablespoon chili powder

Mix cheddar cheese and cream cheese. Add walnuts. Blend in garlic powder, Worcestershire sauce, and minced onion. Shape into ball. Roll in chili powder and refrigerate until well chilled. Make at least 1 day before serving.

Salmon Ball

1 1-pound can red salmon
1 8-ounce package cream
   cheese, softened
1 tablespoon lemon juice
2 teaspoons grated onion

1 teaspoon prepared horseradish
¼ teaspoon salt
¼ teaspoon liquid smoke
½ cup chopped pecans
3 tablespoons chopped parsley

Combine the first seven ingredients. Chill. Shape mixture into ball and roll in pecans and parsley. Serve with crackers.

Appetizer Loaf

½ pound grated sharp cheese
4 tablespoons chopped onion
6 stuffed olives, chopped
4 tablespoons chopped sour
   pickle

2 tablespoons chopped pimento
yolk of 2 hard cooked eggs
½ teaspoon salt
8 tablespoons mayonnaise
1 cup cracker crumbs

Mix well. Roll in waxed paper to form a log. Store in refrigerator overnight. Slice and serve.

Artichoke Dip

2 14-ounce cans artichoke
   hearts, drained & chopped
⅛ teaspoon garlic powder
¾ cup mayonnaise

½ teaspoon Worcestershire
   sauce
1 cup grated Parmesan cheese
dash of pepper

Preheat oven to 350 degrees. Combine all ingredients and bake for 20-25 minutes. Keep warm in chafing dish. Serve with wheat crackers.

Ribbon Sandwiches

Cut crusts from sliced white and whole wheat bread. Stack 2 slices of each bread alternately. Spread with your choice of fillings.

Wrap the sandwiches in waxed paper and chill in the refrigerator. At serving time, cut sandwiches as desired.

Cucumber Sandwiches

Cut sandwich bread slices into rounds. Lightly cover each with 1 teaspoon whipped cream cheese. Fill each two rounds with a thin cucumber slice.

Cheese Spread

2 cups grated cheddar cheese
1 3-ounce package cream
    cheese, softened
¼ cup mayonnaise or salad
    dressing
½ teaspoon Worcestershire
    sauce
⅛ teaspoon onion salt
⅛ teaspoon garlic salt
⅛ teaspoon celery salt

Mix all ingredients thoroughly.

Chicken Olive Spread

3 cups chopped cooked chicken
½ cup finely-chopped celery
¼ cup chopped green olives
½ teaspoon salt
¾ cup mayonnaise or salad
    dressing

Mix all ingredients thoroughly.

Ham Spread

2 cups ground cooked ham
1 can (8¾ ounces) crushed
    pineapple, drained
½ cup finely-chopped celery
½ cup sour cream
¼ teaspoon paprika
⅛ teaspoon salt
⅛ teaspoon pepper
⅛ teaspoon cloves

Mix all ingredients thoroughly.

Spreads for Tea Sandwiches

Cream Spreads

Orange: Blend 1 tablespoon orange juice and 1 tablespoon grated orange peel into a 3-ounce package cream cheese.

Ginger: Soften a 3-ounce package cream cheese with 1 teaspoon milk. Blend in 2 tablespoons finely chopped crystallized ginger and 2 tablespoons finely chopped almonds.

Honey: Blend 1 tablespoon honey and 1 teaspoon lemon juice into a 3-ounce package of whipped cream cheese.

Fruit Cream: Stir 2 tablespoons of jam, jelly, or preserves into a 3-ounce package of softened cream cheese.

Butter Spreads

Almond: Mix ½ cup softened butter with 1 tablespoon finely chopped almonds and ½ teaspoon almond flavoring.

Orange: Mix ½ cup softened butter with 1 tablespoon orange juice and 1 tablespoon grated orange peel.

Open-Face Sandwiches

Hearts — Cut sandwich bread slices into heart shapes with cookie cutter. Lightly cover each with soft butter. Spread each heart with one teaspoon red jam or jelly. If desired, outline edge with whipped cream cheese.

Diamonds — Cut sandwich bread slices into diamond shapes with cookie cutter. Lightly cover each with soft butter. Moisten canned deviled ham with mayonnaise. Spread over diamonds. Garnish with sliced pimento-stuffed olives.

Rounds or Squares — Cut sandwich bread slices into rounds or squares. Spread each with whipped cream cheese (plain, chive, or pimento). Garnish each with a pecan or walnut half.

Pineapple-Nut Sandwiches

¼ cup evaporated milk	1 cup crushed pineapple, drained
2 8-ounce packages softened cream cheese	¼ cup chopped pecans

Blend milk and cream cheese. Add crushed pineapple and nuts. Mix well. Spread between thin slices of orange or raisin bread.

Party Sandwich Loaf

1 small loaf unsliced white bread	Avocado Filling
Softened butter or margarine	8 ounces cream cheese
Ham and Celery Filling	Light cream
Curried Egg Filling	Sliced stuffed olives
	Sprigs of parsley

Cut loaf into four thick slices. Spread each slice with butter. Spread bottom slice with Ham and Celery Filling. Top with second bread slice, and spread with Curried Egg Filling. Top with third bread slice, and spread with Avocado Filling. Top with remaining bread slice. Mash cream cheese. Stir in enough cream so cheese will spread easily. Beat until smooth and spread on top and sides of loaf. Garnish with olive slices and parsley. Slice to serve.

Ham and Celery Filling: Combine 1 cup ground cooked ham, ½ cup finely-chopped celery, and enough mayonnaise to moisten.

Curried Egg Filling: Combine 4 finely-chopped hard-cooked eggs, ½ teaspoon curry powder, and enough mayonnaise to moisten.

Avocado Filling: Mash 2 fully-ripened avocados and add 2 tablespoons French dressing. Stir until well-blended.

BEVERAGES

Mocha Punch

½ cup instant coffee	1 gallon milk
2 cups hot water	½ gallon vanilla ice cream
1 cup sugar	½ gallon chocolate ice cream

Combine coffee, water, and sugar. Prepare in advance and let cool. At serving time, place half the coffee mixture in punch bowl. Add half the milk and half of each flavor of ice cream. Refill with remaining ingredients as needed.

Spiced Cider

2 quarts apple cider	12 whole cloves
½ cup firmly-packed brown sugar	4 cinnamon sticks

Combine in saucepan. Bring to a boil and simmer 5 minutes. Strain. Serve hot in mugs or cups. Yield: 12 servings.

Hot Chocolate Mix

8 quart box powdered milk	½ cup powdered sugar
1 pound box powdered chocolate drink mix	6 ounce jar non-dairy coffee cream

Mix ingredients and store in a tight container. Use ¼ to ½ cup of mix per serving. Add hot water slowly until cup is full and ceases to bubble. Stir. Note: requires a large container for mixing. Yield: 1 gallon of mixture.

Hot Spiced Tea

1 jar (1 lb., 2 ozs.) instant orange breakfast drink
1 12-ounce package lemonade mix
2 cups sugar
1½ teaspoons cloves
3 tablespoons cinnamon
¾ cup instant tea

Mix ingredients thoroughly. Use 2-3 teaspoons per cup of boiling water. Store in glass container.

Tea Punch

Brew 4 small tea bags in 1 quart water.
Add: 1 can (6 ounces) frozen orange juice
1 can (6 ounces) frozen lemonade
1 cup sugar

Dilute juices with water according to directions on can. Mix all ingredients. Yield: 3 quarts.

Hot Fruited Tea

5 cups boiling water
5 small tea bags
10 whole cloves
¼ teaspoon cinnamon
½ cup sugar
¼ cup lemon juice
⅓ cup orange juice
3 unpeeled orange slices, cut in half (if desired)

Pour boiling water over tea, cloves, and cinnamon. Cover and let steep 5 minutes. Strain tea; stir in sugar and fruit juices. Heat to just below boiling. Serve hot with orange slice in each cup. Yield: 6 servings.

Golden Fruit Punch

Frozen juices: 1 can (12 ounces) orange juice
1 can (6 ounces) lemonade
1 can (6 ounces) pineapple juice
2 quarts ginger ale

Dilute with water according to directions on can. Add ginger ale. Yield: 30 servings using punch cups.

Strawberry Punch

2 3-ounce packages strawberry gelatin

2 cups hot water

2 cans (12 ounces each) frozen orange juice

2 cans (6 ounces each) frozen lemon *juice*

3 cans (16 ounces each) pineapple juice

½-ounce bottle almond extract

6 10-ounce bottles ginger ale

Mix ingredients and chill. Yield: 50 servings.

Lime Punch

1 3-ounce package lime gelatin

1 cup hot water

2 cups cold water

1 can (6 ounces) frozen lemonade

1 cup pineapple juice

1 quart ginger ale

Dilute lemonade with water as directed on can. Add ½ cup sugar if using unsweetened pineapple juice. Mix all ingredients and chill. Yield: 15 servings.

Tea Delight

4 cups boiling water

8 small tea bags

2 cups sugar

4 cans (12 ounces each) apricot nectar

1 cup fresh lemon juice

4 cups orange juice

4 cups pineapple juice

3 quarts ginger ale

Add tea bags to boiling water. Brew 5 minutes. Pour into container with sugar and stir until dissolved. Add remaining ingredients except ginger ale. Chill. Add ginger ale just before serving and pour over ice ring in punch bowl. Garnish with lemon or orange slices. May be served hot. Extra water or ginger ale may be added. Yield: 7 quarts.

Hot Cranberry Punch

1 quart cranberry juice cocktail

2 cups pineapple juice

1 cup apricot nectar

2 sticks cinnamon

1 teaspoon allspice

1 teaspoon whole cloves

Pour all juices into coffee maker. Put spices into basket. Allow to go through perk cycle and serve hot. Yield: 15 cups.

Belgian Coffee

1 egg white
⅓ cup sugar
¼ cup whipping cream,
    whipped

4 cups boiling water
2 tablespoons plus 2 teaspoons
    instant coffee

Beat egg white. Gradually add sugar; continue beating until stiff. Fold meringue into whipped cream. Pour boiling water over coffee; stir until coffee dissolves. Place 2 tablespoons mixture into each cup. Fill with coffee. Yield: 10 servings using demitasse or other small cups.

Spiced Coffee

2 cups water
1 tablespoon brown sugar
2 cinnamon sticks

¼ strip orange peel
¼ teaspoon whole allspice
1 tablespoon instant coffee

Combine all ingredients except coffee in saucepan; heat to boiling. Strain mixture; pour liquid over coffee and stir until coffee dissolves. Yield: 4 cups using demitasse or other small cups.

Special Coffee

Serve fresh, hot coffee topped with whipped cream and sprinkled with cinnamon and/or nutmeg.

Hot Mocha

Mix ⅓ cup instant cocoa mix and ¼ cup instant coffee in a serving pot. Pour in 4 cups boiling water; stir. Serve steaming hot and top with sweetened whipped cream. Yield: 8 servings using demitasse or other small cups.

Cafe Au Lait

Simultaneously pour 4 cups hot, strong coffee from one pot and 4 cups hot milk from another into cups. Yield: 8 servings.

SALADS, FRUITS, AND SAUCES

Taos Salad

2 cups shredded lettuce
2 cups red kidney beans, drained
2 medium tomatoes, chopped and drained
1 tablespoon canned green chilies, chopped
½ cup sliced ripe olives
1 large avocado, mashed
½ cup sour cream

2 tablespoons Italian salad dressing
1 teaspoon instant minced onion
¾ teaspoon chili powder
¼ teaspoon salt
½ cup sharp cheddar cheese, shredded
½ cup coarsely crushed corn chips

Combine lettuce, beans, tomatoes, chilies, and olives in salad bowl; chill. For dressing: blend avocado and sour cream. Add Italian dressing, onion, chili powder, salt, and dash pepper. Mix well and chill.

Season salad with salt and pepper to taste. Toss with avocado dressing. Top with cheese and corn chips. Garnish with ripe olives, if desired. Yield: 4-6 servings.

Fresh Fruit Salad

2 medium unpared apples, quartered and cut into ¼ inch slices
1 pound seedless green grapes

2 oranges, pared and sliced
8 lettuce cups
½ cup blueberries

Arrange apple slices, grapes, and orange slices in lettuce cups. Sprinkle with blueberries and cover with Limeade Dressing (see below). To prepare ahead of time, dip apples in dressing and refrigerate. Yield: 8 servings.

Party Melon Boat

1 large watermelon (approximately 30 pounds)
2 medium cantaloupes

1 large honeydew melon
1 quart blueberries

Steps in preparing the melon boat:
1. Cut a 1-inch slice off one side to prevent tipping;
2. With a small knife, make a shallow guide line;
3. With a long, heavy knife, cut off top;

4. With a melon ball cutter, cut out melon from rind;
5. With a large spoon, scrape inside of rind to a smooth surface;
6. Drain liquid;
7. To decorate rind, cut out triangles or scallops along top;
8. Cut cantaloupe and honeydew melons in half cross-wise;
9. With a teaspoon, scrape out seeds;
10. Cut out melon with a melon ball cutter;
11. Place all the melon balls plus blueberries in the watermelon boat; mix gently.

Chill at least 2 hours. Cover with plastic wrap if kept longer. There will probably be enough melon to fill the boat more than once. Yield: 20-25 servings.

Fresh Fruit Tray

Arrange finger-size pieces of chilled watermelon, pineapple, cantaloupe or honeydew melon, bananas, thin unpeeled slices of red apples, and quartered, cored, unpeeled pears on a bed of crisp salad greens. Place a small, whole pineapple in the center of the tray. Provide dressing if desired. (See Fresh Fruit Dip and Limeade Dressing below.)

Fresh Fruit Dip

1 8-ounce package cream cheese
1 7-ounce jar marshmallow creme

Combine softened cream cheese and marshmallow creme; mix until well blended.

Variation: Add 1 tablespoon orange juice and 1 teaspoon grated orange rind to mixture.

Variation: Add 1/8 teaspoon cinnamon, nutmeg, or ground ginger to mixture.

Limeade Dressing

Mix 1/3 cup frozen limeade concentrate (thawed), 1/3 cup honey, and 1/3 cup salad oil.

Sour Cream Sauce

Mix 1 cup sour cream with 2 tablespoons dark brown sugar. Spoon into bowl and sprinkle with a small amount of brown sugar.

Frozen Fruit

Cut fresh fruits (apples, oranges, seedless green grapes, bananas or melon) into bite-size pieces to make 2 cups of fruit. Insert plastic pick into each piece. Melt 6 ounces semi-sweet chocolate pieces and ¼ cup butter in small pan. Dip fruit into chocolate; place on lightly-buttered waxed paper. Freeze fruit until solid (about 3 hours). Yield: 30-36 pieces.

Fruit and Cheese Tray

Arrange a variety of cheeses on an attractive tray. Choose a pleasing variety of tastes and textures; for example, one soft, one semi-soft, and one hard cheese together with mild and sharp cheeses. Fill in tray with your choice of apples, pears, oranges, grapes, and strawberries or raspberries if in season. Dates, prunes, figs, and walnuts may also be added.

CASSEROLES AND ENTREÉS

Chicken Salad

3 cups diced chicken
1½ stalks diced celery
1½ cups seedless grapes, cut in half
¾ cup toasted almonds

3 tablespoons lemon juice
1 cup mayonnaise
¼ cup cream
1½ teaspoons salt
1 teaspoon mustard

Combine chicken, celery, and lemon juice. Chill. Add other ingredients. May be served on cantaloupe rings placed on lettuce leaves. Garnish with additional toasted almonds. Yield: 8-10 servings.

Mexican Casserole

2 pounds ground beef
1 10-ounce can enchilada sauce
1 large onion, chopped
Garlic salt and table salt

1 soup can water
1 can green chili peppers
1-2 packages frozen tortillas
1 pound sharp cheese, grated

Brown meat and onion. Add sauce and salts. Heat soup and chilies. Layer in 9″×13″ baking dish in the following order: tortillas, meat, soup, cheese; then repeat. Refrigerate overnight. Bake 1 hour at 350 degrees. Yield: 8 servings.

Marinated Eye of the Round

1 (5 pound) eye of the round roast
¼ cup salad oil
2 tbsp. lemon-pepper seasoning
½ cup wine vinegar
½ cup lemon juice
½ cup soy sauce
½ cup Worcestershire sauce

Mix oil, lemon pepper, vinegar, lemon juice, soy sauce, and Worcestershire sauce. Marinate roast in mixture for 1-3 days, turning at least once per day. Cook uncovered with marinade at 250 degrees for 3 hours. Refrigerate overnight. Slice thinly. Serve with heated marinade if desired. Garnish with parsley and cherry tomatoes. Freezes well. Yield: 10-15 servings.

Wild Rice Casserole

1 cup wild rice
1 10-ounce can condensed consommé
Salt and pepper to taste
1 tablespoon butter
½ pound mushrooms sauteéd in butter

Wash rice carefully. Place in a shallow 1½ quart baking dish and cover with consommé. Let stand 3 hours, then bake covered at 350 degrees for about 45 minutes. Add small amount of water if rice becomes too dry. Add butter and mushrooms. Lightly mix with a fork. Uncover rice and lower oven temperature to 300 degrees. Cook until all liquid is absorbed. Yield: 4 servings.

Green Vegetables With Sauce

1 package frozen green peas
1 package frozen baby lima beans
1 package frozen cut green beans

Sauce:
¾ cup mayonnaise
2 tablespoons salad oil
1 small onion, finely chopped
2 hard-cooked eggs
½ teaspoon prepared mustard
½ teaspoon Worcestershire sauce
Dash tabasco sauce

Cook vegetables separately; drain and mix. Add sauce and heat. May be served cold — if so, do not heat sauce with beans.

BREADS

Applesauce Muffins

1 stick margarine or butter
1 cup sugar
1 egg
¾ teaspoon vanilla
2 cups plain flour
1½ teaspoons cinnamon
1 teaspoon allspice
½ teaspoon cloves
½ teaspoon salt
½ cup chopped nuts
½ cup raisins
1 cup applesauce
1 teaspoon soda

Cream together butter, sugar, egg, and vanilla. Sift flour and spices and add with nuts and raisins to the butter mixture. Combine applesauce and soda. Mix all ingredients thoroughly. Store covered in the refrigerator, preferably 2-3 days before baking. To cook, bake at 400 degrees for 20-25 minutes in greased muffin tins or paper baking cups. Dough keeps for 2-3 weeks in refrigerator. Yield: 12 large muffins.

Whole Wheat Coffee Cake

1 cup boiling water
1 8-oz. package chopped dates
¾ cup sifted self-rising flour
¾ cup whole wheat flour
½ cup brown sugar, packed
⅓ cup sugar
½ cup (1 stick) softened butter
    or margarine
2 eggs
1½ teaspoons vanilla

Pour boiling water over dates; stir. Set aside to cool. Heat oven to 375 degrees. Grease and flour a 9-inch square cake pan. Combine flours and sugars in mixing bowl. Cut in butter with a pastry blender until mixture resembles coarse crumbs. Add date mixture, eggs, and vanilla. Stir until mixture is just blended. Pour batter into prepared pan. Bake 35-40 minutes or until cake pulls away from sides of pan. Remove from oven and pour Pecan Glaze (recipe below) over cake while hot. Cool 10-15 minutes. Cut into squares.

Note: If using plain flour, add 1½ teaspoons baking powder and 1 teaspoon salt. Recipe may be doubled and baked in a 10-inch tube pan for 55-60 minutes. Cool 30 minutes and glaze.

Pecan Glaze

1½ cups confectioner's sugar
3 tablespoons milk
1 teaspoon vanilla
½ teaspoon almond flavoring
½ cup chopped pecans

Combine all ingredients except pecans. Stir until smooth; then stir in pecans.

Orange Tea Bread

3 cups sifted flour
4 teaspoons baking powder
¾ teaspoon salt
½ cup soft shortening
1 egg

½ cup milk
½ cup orange juice
1 medium orange, diced
1 cup sugar

Sift flour, baking powder, and salt into mixing bowl. Place shortening, egg and milk in blender. Add unpeeled, diced orange (about 12 pieces) removing large seeds. Add sugar. Cover and blend about one minute. Pour over sifted mixture. Mix until flour is just moistened. Grease two 7×4 inch loaf pans. Divide equally and bake at 325 degrees for 50 minutes. Cool and let stand overnight before slicing.

Note: A blender is imperative.

Cheese Bread

3 cups biscuit mix
1½ cups grated, sharp cheddar
   cheese
1 tablespoon sugar
1¼ cups milk

1 egg, lightly beaten
1 tablespoon vegetable oil
½ teaspoon dillweed
½ teaspoon dry mustard

Preheat oven to 350 degrees. Generously grease 9×5 inch loaf pan or 6-cup Bundt pan. Combine biscuit mix, cheese, and sugar in large bowl. Combine remaining ingredients in second bowl and mix well. Stir into dry mixture, blending thoroughly, then beat slightly to remove lumps. Turn into pan and bake until golden, 45 to 50 minutes. May be served hot or cold. Yield: 14-17 servings.

Cottage Cheese Pancakes

4 eggs
1 cup cottage cheese
½ cup bran cereal, whole
   wheat flour, or wheat germ

1 tablespoon oil
1 tablespoon honey
1 teaspoon vanilla
Dash of salt

Put ingredients in blender and mix well. Bake on hot, lightly-oiled griddle. Note: can be frozen after cooking. Yield: 4 servings.

Waffles

2 cups sifted flour (plain or
    whole wheat)
1 teaspoon salt
4 teaspoons baking powder

3 eggs
1½ cups milk
½ cup melted butter

Sift dry ingredients. Add beaten eggs, milk, and melted butter. Bake on waffle iron according to instructions for your machine. Yield: 6 waffles.

Variations:

Pecan Waffles: add ½ cup chopped pecans. Serve with honey butter (mix 1 cup soft butter with 1 cup honey) and warm maple syrup.

Easy Belgian Waffles: combine 2 tablespoons confectioner's sugar with 1 cup whipped cream. Fold in 1 cup sliced fresh strawberries. Place topping on waffle and sprinkle with sifted confectioner's sugar.

DESSERTS

Strawberry Tarts

1 cup softened margarine
1 package (8 ounces) cream
    cheese, softened
2 cups sifted flour

Strawberry jam
Chopped pecans

Blend margarine and cream cheese. Gradually add flour and mix well. Chill at least 1 hour. Pinch off small pieces of dough and place in miniature muffin tins, molding them into shells. Add small amount of jam to each shell and top with pecans. Bake at 375 degrees for 20-25 minutes or until shells are light tan color. Remove and cool on wire rack. Note: cherry or apricot preserves may be used instead of strawberry. Yield: 60 servings.

Party Mints

1 box powdered sugar
¾ stick butter
2 tablespoons cream

7 drops food coloring (any color)
12 drops peppermint oil

Melt butter over low heat, add cream, coloring, and oil. Mix in sugar. Blend until smooth. Place into mint molds until firm.

Party Candy

2 egg whites
2½ cups confectioner's sugar, sifted

1 teaspoon vanilla or other flavoring
Food coloring, if desired

Beat egg whites slightly. Add sugar, a small amount at a time, until stiff enough to knead. Stir in flavoring and food coloring. Form candy into desired shapes.

Wedding Cookies

¼ cup sugar
1 cup butter
2 cups flour

1 teaspoon vanilla
¼ teaspoon salt
1 cup finely-chopped pecans

Cream together sugar and butter. Add flour, vanilla, and salt. Stir in pecans. Chill dough. Roll dough into small balls, and make a thumbprint in each of them. Place on ungreased baking sheet and place in 300-degree oven for 20-30 minutes. Remove to cooling rack and fill each thumbprint with frosting of desired color. Yield: 36.

Frosting: Combine 1 cup confectioner's sugar with ½ teaspoon almond flavoring and just enough water to make it the right consistency to spread. Add food coloring.

Variation: Roll dough into small balls and bake as directed above, then roll in confectioner's sugar.

Variation: Place small amount of jelly (any flavor) in each thumbprint and top with a pecan half before baking. Let cool and dust with powdered sugar.

Tea Cakes

1 egg, slightly beaten
1 cup butter
1 cup sugar
2 teaspoons soda
4 tablespoons buttermilk

1 teaspoon vanilla, lemon, or almond flavoring
3-4 cups flour
Pinch of nutmeg (if desired)

Cream sugar and butter. Add egg. Stir in other ingredients, and enough flour to make soft dough. Roll thin on floured board and cut into desired shapes. Use spatula to lift from board to greased pan. Sprinkle cookies with sugar (plain or decorator) or with cinnamon-sugar mixture before baking. Bake until slightly brown, about 10 minutes at 325 degrees. Note: dough may roll easier if chilled.

Dough may be rolled in waxed paper, then frozen, and sliced and baked later. Yield: about 7 dozen cookies.

Heart Meringues

3 egg whites, room temperature 1 teaspoon white vinegar
½ teaspoon cream of tartar ½ teaspoon vanilla flavoring
1 cup sugar

Combine egg whites and cream of tartar. Beat until soft peaks form. Gradually add sugar, beating constantly. Add vinegar and vanilla, beating until stiff peaks form. Tint pink with 5 or 6 drops red food coloring, if desired. Make 8 mounds of ⅓ to ½ cup each on heavy brown paper on baking sheet. Make each into heart shape with back of spoon. Bake in preheated 250-degree oven for 1 hour. Turn off heat and let stand in oven until cool. Just before serving, fill shells with strawberry or vanilla ice cream. Garnish with fresh strawberries. Yield: 8 servings.

Brown Sugar Pound Cake

1 cup butter or margarine 3½ cups sifted flour
½ cup shortening 1 teaspoon baking powder
1 box (1 pound) plus 1 cup 1 cup milk
    light brown sugar 2 teaspoons rum or vanilla
5 eggs   flavoring

Preheat oven to 325 degrees. Cream butter, shortening, and sugar. Add eggs, one at a time, beating well after each addition. Add flour, sifted with baking powder, alternately with milk. Add flavoring. Bake in greased paper-lined 9-inch tube pan for 1 hour and 20 minutes. Yield: 24 servings.

Cherry Torte

½ cup softened butter 1 cup sugar
5 tbsp. confectioner's sugar ¼ teaspoon salt
1 cup cake flour ¼ cup flour
1 can (1 pound) sour cherries, ¾ teaspoon baking powder
    pitted ½ cup chopped nuts
2 eggs, beaten 1 teaspoon vanilla flavoring

Sauce: 1 tablespoon corn starch
Cherry juice ¼ cup sugar

Grease a 9″×13″ baking dish. Cream butter with sugar and flour.

Pat mixture on bottom of dish and bake in 350-degree oven for 15 minutes. Drain cherries, reserving juice for a cherry sauce topping, and combine with remaining ingredients. Pour over the crust and bake 30 minutes at 300-325 degrees. Thicken cherry juice with 1 tablespoon corn starch. Cook until thick. Cut torte into squares, top with sweetened whipped cream and cherry sauce.

Make-Your-Own-Sundae

Chocolate sauce
Butterscotch sauce
Sliced strawberries
Raspberries
Crushed pineapple

Ripe bananas
Assorted nuts
Maraschino cherries
Whipped cream
Assorted flavors of ice cream

Arrange sauces, fruits, and garnishes in serving dishes around containers of ice cream. Have ice cream scoops and sundae dishes ready for each guests to prepare his/her favorite combination.

Sugar Cookies

2 cups sugar
1 cup butter
3 eggs
1 cup sour cream
1 teaspoon soda

1 teaspoon vanilla flavoring
1 teaspoon lemon or almond
    flavoring
4 cups flour

Mix butter and sugar. Add eggs, cream, soda, and flavoring, then add flour. If more flour is needed to make the dough easier to handle, use as little as possible. Roll out the cookies, cut into desired shapes, decorate, and bake on a greased cookie sheet at 375 degrees until light brown.

Strawberry Parfait

1 can (6 ounces) frozen
    lemonade concentrate

1 cup strawberries
1 quart vanilla ice cream

Combine strawberries and lemonade concentrate. Alternate layers of strawberry mixture and ice cream in parfait glasses, starting and ending with strawberry mixture. These can be made days ahead of a party and placed in the freezer. Just before serving, garnish with whipped cream and a strawberry.

Apricot Cake

1 stick butter
1½ cups apricots
½ pound crushed vanilla
    wafers

½ pint whipped cream
1 cup powdered sugar
2 eggs

Cream butter and sugar; add beaten egg yolks and fold in beaten egg whites. Grease pan. Divide crumbs. Line pan with half of the crumbs, pour in mixture, add apricots, then add whipped cream. Pour on remaining crumbs. Refrigerate several hours before serving.

Orange Loaf

2 envelopes unflavored gelatin
½ cup cold water
3 cups orange juice, divided
½ cup sugar
1 pint orange sherbet, slightly
    softened

24 ladyfingers
½ cup whipping cream
2 tablespoons powdered sugar
Mint leaves
Orange slices

In large bowl, sprinkle gelatin over cold water; let stand 3 minutes. In small saucepan, combine 1 cup orange juice and sugar; stir over low heat until sugar dissolves. Add to softened gelatin; stir until gelatin is completely dissolved. Add remaining 2 cups orange juice. Beat sherbet into gelatin mixture with whisk until completely smooth. Chill, stirring often until mixture mounds when dropped from a spoon (will occur quickly because sherbet is cold). Line bottom of 9×5×3 inch loaf pan with 8 split ladyfingers. Spread with one-third of the orange mixture. Repeat layers. Chill 3 hours, or until firm. Whip cream with sugar. Unmold loaf onto serving plate. Frost with whipped cream. Garnish with mint leaves and orange slices. Makes 8 servings.

Blueberry Torte

½ cup butter or margarine
1 cup sugar
3 eggs
¾ cup milk
2 cups fresh or frozen
    blueberries
1½ cups graham cracker
    crumbs

1 cup flour
1 teaspoon baking powder
1 teaspoon soda
Additional blueberries for
    garnish
Whipped cream

Cream butter and add sugar. Beat in eggs, one at a time. Stir in milk. Combine blueberries, graham cracker crumbs, flour, baking powder, and soda. Add all at once and beat until batter is smooth. Pour into a greased 8-inch spring form baking pan. Bake in a preheated 375 degree oven for 50 minutes to an hour or until top is richly browned. Before serving, arrange blueberries over top of cake and garnish with whipped cream.

Toffee Squares

1 cup butter or margarine
1 cup dark brown sugar
1 egg yolk

1 teaspoon vanilla
2 cups sifted, all-purpose flour

Cream butter and brown sugar until fluffy. Beat in egg yolk and vanilla. Add flour. Mix well. This will be a very sticky dough. Spread in greased 9×13 inch pan. Bake at 350 degrees for 15 to 20 minutes.

Topping:

6-ounce package semi-sweet chocolate chips
1 cup finely chopped nuts

Sprinkle chocolate chips on cookie surface while warm. Spread and top with nuts. Cut into squares when cool.

Neapolitan Squares

Bottom Layer:

1¼ cups graham cracker
    crumbs
½ cup melted butter or
    margarine

½ cup brown sugar
⅓ cup all-purpose flour

Combine ingredients. Press lightly into 9×9 inch pan with greased sides. Bake in 350 degree oven for ten minutes.

Second Layer:

2 cups ground coconut
1 can (14 ounces) sweetened, condensed milk

Combine coconut with condensed milk. Spread over bottom layer. Bake in 350 degree oven for 20 minutes or until slightly browned. Allow to cool before frosting.

Icing:

2 cups powdered sugar
4 tablespoons butter or margarine
3 tablespoons juice from maraschino cherries

Beat all together, adding more juice, if needed, to make icing soft enough to spread. Spread over cooled bars. Cover tightly and store at least one day. Cut into squares before serving.

This is an attractive addition to a plate of squares and keeps well.

Party Cheesecakes

1 pound cream cheese
2 eggs
¾ cup sugar

1 tablespoon lemon juice
1 teaspoon vanilla
Vanilla wafers
Miniature foil baking cups

Topping: Mix 1 can cherry pie filling with 1 teaspoon almond flavoring.

Blend cream cheese, eggs, sugar, lemon juice and vanilla. Place a vanilla wafer in bottom of each miniature foil baking cup. Pour creamed cheese mixture over the wafer, filling ½ to ⅔ full. Bake 15 to 20 minutes in 375 degree oven. Cool. Place 1 tablespoon topping on each. These freeze well but cannot be stored for long periods of time in the refrigerator. Yield: 18-24 servings.

Easy Elegant Easter Eggs

1 stick butter or margarine
1 teaspoon vanilla

⅔ cup sweetened condensed milk
6 cups confectioner's sugar

Cream butter until light and fluffy. Add vanilla and condensed milk; beat until blended. Add 2 cups sugar and mix well. Keep adding 2 cups and blending until 6 cups are used. Remove the mixture to a clean work surface and knead until a smooth consistency.

Butter Cream: Shape 2 tablespoons mixture into an egg form; dip in melted chocolate (melted chocolate chips).

Coconut: Add desired amount of coconut to mixture and proceed as for butter cream.

Fruit/Nut: Add chopped candied fruit and/or nuts to mixture; proceed as for butter cream.

Peanut Butter: Wrap butter cream mixture around a small amount of peanut butter to form an egg. Dip into melted chocolate.

Raspberry Parfait

Into parfait glasses, put alternate layers of vanilla or eggnog ice cream and frozen raspberries, starting with ice cream and ending with berries. May be made a day ahead and stored in the freezer. Just before serving, top each parfait with whipped cream and additional berries.

Sherbet Balls

With small scoop make sherbet balls from 1 quart each of lime, lemon and raspberry sherbet. Place on baking sheet or waxed paper; freeze. At serving time, alternate colored sherbet balls in glass serving bowl or individual sherbet glasses. Makes 12 servings. Serve with tea cakes or wedding cookies (included in this section.)

Chocolate Cream Dessert

6 ounce package semi-sweet chocolate pieces	18 ladyfingers, split
6 eggs, separated	1 cup whipping cream, chilled
1½ teaspoons vanilla	2 tbsp. confectioner's sugar
	2 tbsp. cocoa

Melt chocolate in the top of a double boiler. Add egg yolks, one at a time, beating well after each addition. Add vanilla and stir well. Beat egg whites until stiff. Fold in chocolate mixture.

Line a loaf pan with waxed paper, allowing it to extend over top edges of pan. Place a layer of ladyfingers on the bottom and around the sides of pan. Spoon in half the chocolate mixture. Top with another layer of ladyfingers; spoon in remaining chocolate mixture and top with remaining ladyfingers. Chill several hours or until firm.

Just before serving, whip the cream. Fold in cocoa and confectioner's sugar. Lift dessert from pan; place on serving dish. Remove paper. Frost with whipped cream mixture. Makes 8 servings.

Garnishes

• Arrange flowers and leaves around the outside of your punch bowl.

• Arrange frosted grapes to drape over the edge of a punch bowl. To frost grapes, dip small clusters into beaten egg white and then into granulated sugar. Dry frosted grapes on a wire rack.

- Float thin slices of lemon, orange, lime, or whole strawberries on fruit punches.
- Freeze juice or punch in ring, bell, or heart-shaped molds. Add to punch bowl immediately before serving. Cookie cutters may also be used for seasonal motifs or special themes.
- Make a Della Robbia ice ring to carry out the Christmas theme. Use a ring mold or a tube pan and a variety of small fruits, such as cherries, small bunches of grapes, strawberries, raspberries, cranberries, small limes, apricots, or plums. Also, add mint, holly, or lemon leaves. Wash fruit and leaves well.

Arrange a layer of fruit and leaves, top side down in the mold. Pour in ice water to a depth of ¾ inch. Some of the fruit will not be covered with water. Freeze. Quickly arrange another layer of fruit and pour in another layer of ice water. Freeze. Repeat until mold is filled. To use, unmold and put bottom side up, in the bowl of punch.

- Use fresh flowers to garnish dessert trays and parsley to garnish vegetable and meat dishes.
- Use radish rosettes and cherry tomatoes to garnish snack or sandwich trays.
- Arrange mandarin orange segments around the base of a frosted layer cake. Garnish top of cake with a flower of orange segments and a maraschino cherry.
- For a special luncheon or dinner, decorate each butter pat with a sprig of parsley. Butter can also be formed into curls or balls. Drop curls and balls into iced water, cover and refrigerate until serving time.

Suggested Gifts

The selection of a shower gift for the bride-to-be is a basic question. Intelligent choices of gifts by her friends are invaluable in providing her with the things she really needs. The following lists will help hostesses as well as guests make good gift choices, and will also be useful to the bride-to-be herself.

Select neutral colors in gifts unless you know the bride's color scheme, and always try to select items that will be used often. Consider buying expensive items jointly with other guests. Buy gifts that both the bride and groom can use (unless it is a personal shower gift), and don't forget to consider a gift of flowers, fruit, cheese, or meat delivered weekly, monthly, or on special occasions. Purchase bed linens only if you know the kind of bed the couple has chosen — double, queen, king, or waterbed. Purchase exchangeable items in the event that the bride receives duplicate gifts, and above all purchase tasteful gifts only: avoid "bizarre" or outlandish presents.

Gifts of flatware should always be in the bride's chosen pattern. The following list applies to both the bride's formal and informal selections.

Flatware

- Teaspoons
- Knives
- Forks
- Salad forks
- Soup spoons
- 3 tablespoons (one of which should be slotted)
- Gravy ladle
- Butter knife
- Cold meat fork
- Cake or pie server
- Iced tea spoons
- Pickle fork
- Sugar spoon

Hollow Ware

- Candle sticks
- Water pitcher
- Bread tray
- Gravy boat
- Salt and pepper shakers
- Trays
- Casseroles
- Compotes
- Napkin holders
- Bud vases

Formal China and Casual Dinnerware

- Dinner plates
- Bread and butter plates
- Cups and saucers
- Salad plates
- Cereal dishes (use for soups, puddings, fruit)
- Sugar bowl
- Cream pitcher
- Vegetable dish
- Gravy boat
- Platters

Crystal and Informal Glassware

- Goblets
- Iced beverage glasses
- Sherbet glasses
- Dessert/salad plates

Kitchen Equipment

Gifts for the kitchen are grouped according to their function. The list below suggests items which are useful and which might not be considered otherwise.

- Can opener (electric and manual)
- Vegetable brush
- Garnish cutters
- Fruit juicer
- Carrot peeler
- Collander
- Jar opener
- Knife holder
- Knife sharpener
- Spatulas
- Kitchen shears
- Apple corer
- Grapefruit knife
- Metal measuring cups
- Glass measuring cup
- Set of measuring spoons
- Flour sifter
- Mixing bowls
- Mixing spoons
- Wire whisks
- Biscuit cutter
- Rolling pin
- Bowl scraper
- Strainers
- Cookie cutters
- Pastry brush
- Molds (various shapes and sizes)
- Salt and pepper shakers
- Omelet pan
- Steamer

- Tea kettle
- Long-handled fork and spoon
- Egg poacher
- Baking pans (pie, cake and muffin)
- Roaster
- Cookie sheets
- Crock pot
- Tube pan
- Loaf pan
- Coffee maker
- Toaster oven
- Teapot
- Electric knife
- Serving trays
- Paper towel holder
- Waste basket
- Baking dishes
- Canister set
- Cutlery set
- Cutting board
- Covered casseroles (various sizes)
- Double boiler
- Food processor
- Saucepans (various sizes)
- Skillets
- Wok
- Blender
- Waffle iron
- Crepe pan
- Ice cream freezer

Cleaning Equipment

- Vacuum cleaner (upright and hand-held)
- Carpet sweeper
- Mops
- Brooms
- Dustpan
- High quality polishes and waxes (furniture, leather, silver, brass)
- Brushes

Linens

Table
- Tablecloths
- Napkins
- Place mats

Kitchen
- Dish towels
- Dish cloths
- Potholders
- Hand towels
- Aprons
- Hot pads
- Mitts

Bed
- Bedspreads
- Blankets
- Mattress pads
- Pillowcases
- Pillow covers
- Sheets
- Blanket covers
- Comforters
- Lightweight blankets
- Electric blanket

Bath

- Bath mats
- Bath towels
- Hand towels
- Guest towels
- Wash cloths
- Shower curtain

Laundry Equipment

- Iron
- Ironing board
- Ironing pad and cover
- Clothes hamper
- Clothes basket

Other Gifts and Decorative Accessories

- Salad bowl and servers (wood or glass)
- Bread basket
- Condiment dishes (glass, china, or pottery)
- Water pitcher
- Coffee pot for serving (not a coffee maker)
- Ice cream dishes
- Electric warming tray
- Steak knives
- Baskets
- Bowls
- Candlesticks
- Clock
- Figurines
- Mirrors
- Decorative pillows
- Gourmet items
- Books (address book, guest book, coupon organizer, photo album, cookbooks)
- Stationery
- Gardening supplies
- Hobby and game equipment

Bridal Shower Planning Guide

Hostess: _____

_____

Guest(s) of Honor: _____

_____

_____

_____

Theme: _____

_____

Invitations: _____

    Date:_____

    Time: _____

    Place: _____

    Other Information: _____

_____

_____

Decorations: _____

_____

_____

_____

_____

Entertainment: _____

_____

_____

_____

_____

Presentation of Gifts: _____

_____

_____

_____

_____

_____

Guests: _____

_____

_____

_____

_____

_____

_____

_____

_____

_____

_____

_____

_____

_____

_____

_____

_____

_____

_____

_____

_____

_____

Menu and Recipes: _____

_____

_____

_____

_____

_____

_____

_____

_____

_____

_____

_____

_____

_____

_____

_____

_____

_____

_____

_____